The Land They Loved

Volume I

Portraits:

Top Left: Edgar Allan Poe

Top Right: Albert Pike

Center: William Gilmore Simms

Bottom Left: Mirabeau Lamar

Bottom Right: Francis Scott Key

The Land They Loved:

Volume I
Southern Poets And Poems,
1606 -1860

Edited by
Clyde N. Wilson

Southern Poets And Poems, 1606 -1860:
The Land They Loved Volume 1

Produced in the Republic of South Carolina by

SHOTWELL PUBLISHING LLC

Post Office Box 2592

Columbia, So. Carolina 29202

www.ShotwellPublishing.com

Cover Design: Boo Jackson. Portraits are public domain courtesy of
Library of Congress, Texas State Library, National Portrait Gallery and Wikimedia.

ISBN: 978-1-963506-14-3

FIRST EDITION

10 9 8 7 6 5 4 3 2

Contents

Foreword

THIS COLLECTION IS MADE, not from the viewpoint of a critic of literature, but that of a student of history interested in how the experiences of the Southern people have been reflected in verse. This collection is made in the belief that poetry conveys a kind of truth not found in other forms of human discourse. Of course, such a sample cannot give a full account of the quality and range of such world-class Southern geniuses in poetry as Poe, Simms, Warren, Ransom, Davidson, Middleton, Chappell, and Berry.

Poetry, of course, is akin to music — music in words. Mostly formal verse is collected here, although it should not be overlooked that a great deal of Southern (and American) life and spirit is reflected in the Southern popular songs of the 19th and 20th centuries, among which gospel, a subject in itself, is an important part. We have only occasionally looked into those realms, although without exception every original and important form of American music has its origins in the South and reflects the Southern spirit. Southern "country music" was the only natural and creative source of American lyrics in the later 20th century. (At least until it was commercialised by people who wish to profit from Southern creativity without understanding or acknowledging it.)

Occasionally we have included documents that are not verse but that have poetic sentiments about Southern people and events.

Southern verse presents an astounding proof of what the South has meant to many good and intelligent people over many generations.

The Alabama poet Alexander Beaufort Meek wrote in the Preface to his *Songs and Poems of the South* in 1857:

> The Poetry of a country should be a faithful expression of its physical and moral characteristics. The imagery, at least, should be drawn from the indigenous objects of the region, and the sentiments be such as naturally arise under the influence of its climate, its institutions, habits of life, and social condition. Verse, so fashioned and coloured, is as much the genuine product and growth of a Land, as its trees or flowers. It partakes of the raciness of the soil, the purity of the atmosphere, the brilliancy of its skies, its mountain pictures, and its broad sweeps of level and undulating territory. The Scenery infuses itself into the Song; and the feelings and fancies are modulated by the circumstances amid which they had their birth.
>
> These opinions have formed the poetic Faith of the writer of the present volume. He has not attempted to sing in a mere spirit of imitativeness, or in the tropes and metaphors of foreign Art and Precedent. Gazing upon the delightful Land about him-the Land of his birth and affections—he has endeavored to depict its beauties,—to weave its illustrative objects into the tissues of his imagination, and to give utterance to the thoughts and emotions congenial to a mind impressed by such associations, and loving at once the Patriotic and the Beautiful.

William Gilmore Simms, the father of Southern literature, expressed similar ideas in his preface to *War Poetry of the South*:

> The emotional literature of a people is as necessary to the philosophical historian as the mere details of events in the progress of a nation. This is essential to the

reputation of the Southern people, as illustrating their feelings, sentiments, ideas and opinions—-the motives which influenced their actions, and the objects which they had in contemplation, and which seemed to them to justify the struggle in which they were engaged.

Our poets certainly deal with many of the primary ingredients of Southern experience. First, the surrounding wilderness, which has been a theatre of Southern life from 1607 to the present. To a surprising extent the poets are attracted by one of the denizens of unsettled spaces—the spirited mocking bird. Also to another denizen, the Native American. Pinkney, Meek, and Simms deal with these original people with chivalric sympathy and respect that is not very common with Northern writers. And other common themes: Christian faith, love of home places and home States, courage in defense of liberty, warning against a materialist view of life, and of course, the universal theme of modern verse, personal sentiments and emotions.

There is or used to be a long-established mainstream generalisation that the Old South was poor and backward in literature, except possibly for oratory. This idea was established by the busy self-promoting scribblers of New England who considered themselves the only true Americans and who had a free field after the South was impoverished by the War and Reconstruction. The lie about the intellectual inferiority of the Old South has been refuted conclusively by serious historians in recent years.

Henry Timrod in an antebellum essay on Southern literature pointed out, with gentlemanly avoidance of boasting, that Southern writing in his time showed merit but had not quite reached universal and timeless status. Our poets show learning and understanding that is certainly unsurpassed by the literature northeast of the Hudson. Poe, Simms, and the writers known as "Southwestern humourists" stand in fiction among the high rank of American writers. Poe, Simms, Timrod, and other poets presaged a literature that would achieve undoubted universal status in the 20th century. The 19th century wounded but did not kill the Southern soul.

I. Foundations

MICHAEL DRAYTON (1563 — 1631), English Renaissance poet, never came to the New World. In 1606 he wrote this ode "To the Virginian Voyage," in honour of Sir Walter Raleigh's first expedition to plant a permanent settlement of English people in North America. The poem illustrates the culture out of which the first Southerners came and almost uncannily anticipates the South that was soon to be founded. Spelling has been somewhat modernised for clarity.

Ode To The Virginian Voyage

You brave heroic minds,

Worthy your country's name,

That honour still pursue,

Go and subdue,

Whilst loitering hinds

Lurk here at home with shame.

Britons, you stay too long;

Quickly aboard bestow you,

And with a merry gale

Swell your stretch'd sail,

With vows as strong

As the winds that blow you.

Your course securely steer,

West and by south forth keep,

Rocks, lee-shores, nor shoals,

When AEolus scowls

You need not fear,

So absolute the deep.

And cheerfully at sea,

Success you still entice,

To get the pearl and gold,
And ours to hold Virginia,
Earth's only paradise.

Where nature hath in store
Fowl, venison, and fish,
And the fruitfull'st soil
Without your toil
Three harvests more,
All greater than your wish.

And the ambitious vine
Crowns with his purple mass,
The cedar reaching high
To kiss the sky,
The cypress, pine,
And useful sassafras.

To whose the Golden Age,
Still nature's laws doth give,
No other cares tend,
But them to defend
From winter's rage,
That long there doth not live.

When as the luscious smell
Of that delicious land,
Above the seas that flows,
The clear wind throws,

Your hearts to swell
Approaching the dear strand,
In kenning of the shore
Thanks to God first given,
O you the happi'st men,
Be frolic then,
Let cannons roar,
Frighting the wide heaven.

And in regions far,
Such heroes bring ye forth
As those from whom we came
And plant our name
Under that star
Not known unto our north.

And as there plenty grows
Of laurel everywhere,
Apollo's sacred tree,
You it may see
A poet's brows
To crown, that may sing there.
Thy voyages attend
Industrious Hakluyt,
Whose reading shall enflame
Men to seek fame,
And much commend
To after times thy wit.

◆ ◆ ◆

JOHN COTTON (fl. 1660s — 1720s) was an early settler of Virginia, never to be confused with the awful Cotton family of Massachusetts. In 1814 an anonymous poem about Bacon's Rebellion in Virginia (1676) was found among some old mss. and subsequently published. It was long regarded as an anonymous treasure of American colonial literature. Twentieth-century poet and critic Louis Untermeyer called it the best thing written in America in the 17th century, said that "it is one of the noblest anonymous elegies we possess" and was "our first indubitable [American] poem." Not until 1937 was the author identified and a complete text assembled due to the painstaking work of the great scholar of Southern literature, Prof. Jay B. Hubbell of Duke University. He identified the author as John Cotton I of Stafford County, Virginia, who was a participant in Bacon's Rebellion, but I cannot help but feel a suspicion that the writer may be a woman. The poem is presented here with incidentals modernised.

Bacon's Epitaph, Made by His Man

Death, why so cruel? What no other way

To manifest thy spleen but thus to slay

Our hopes of safety, liberty, our all,

Which through thy tyranny with him must fall

To its late chaos? Had thy rigid force

Been dealt by retail and not thus in gross,

Grief had been silent. Now we must complain

Since thou in him hast more than thousands slain

Whose lives and safeties did so much depend

On him, their life, with him their lives must end.

If 't be a sin to think Death bribed can be,

We must be guilty. Say 'twas bribery

Guided the fatal shaft. Virginia's foes,

To whom for secret crimes just vengeance owes

Deserved plagues, dreading their just desert,
Corrupted Death by Paracelsian art
Him to destroy; whose well-tried courage such
Their heartless hearts, nor arms, nor strength could touch.

Who now must heal those wounds or stop that blood
The heathen made and drew into a flood?
Who is't must plead our cause? Nor trump nor drum
Nor deputations; these alas! are dumb
And cannot speak. Our arms, though ne'er so strong,
Will want the aid of his commanding tongue,
Which conquered more than Caesar. He o'erthrew
Only the outward frame; this could subdue
The rugged works of nature. Souls replete
With dull chill cold he'd animate with heat
Drawn forth of reason's limbec. In a word,
Mars and Minerva both in him concurred
For arts, for arms, whose pen and sword alike,
As Cato's did, may admiration strike
Into his foes, while they confess withal
It was their guilt styled him a criminal.

Only this difference does from truth proceed:
They in the guilt, he in the name must bleed,
While none shall dare his obsequies to sing
In deserved measures until time shall bring
Truth crowned with freedom and from danger free
To sound his praises to posterity.

Here let him rest, while we this truth report:
He's gone from hence unto a higher court
To plead his cause, where he by this doth know
Whether to Caesar he was friend or foe.

♦ ♦ ♦

EBENEZER COOKE (fl. *ca.* 1680s — 1730s?) of Maryland is a major figure in Colonial American literature. He is best known for the long satirical poem "The Sot-Weed Factor." The sot-weed is tobacco, mainstay of the Southern and American economy in the colonial period, and the factor is a figure long familiar in the South—the merchant who sold and exported the plantations' tobacco, cotton, or rice, and shipped to the plantation purchased goods. (A Yankee writer named Barth in the 20[th]century appropriated Cooke's title for a novel.) The first item is from "The Sot-Weed Factor" (1708) and the second is a preface to Cooke's long poem "The Maryland Muse" (1731). Cooke shows the humorous and positive spirit of the South at a time when the literature of New England consisted entirely of Puritan cant.

While riding near a Sandy Bay,

I met a Quaker, Yea and Nay;

A Pious Conscientious Rogue,

As e'er woar Bonnet or a Brogue,

Who neither Swore nor kept his Word,

But cheated in the Fear of God;

And when his Debts he would not pay,

By Light within he ran away.

♦

Old poet,

As you may remember,

You told me sometime in September

Your pleasant Muse was idly sitting,

Longing for some new Subject fitting

For this Meridian, and her Inditing,

Worth Praise and Pence for Pains in Writing.

I therefore (thinking it great Pity

A Muse should pine, that is so witty)

Have sent an old, authentic Book,

For Her in Doggrel Verse to Cook;

For since it never was in Print,

(Tho' wondrous Truths are written in't)

It may be worthy Clio's Rhimes,

To hand it down to future Times.

◆ ◆ ◆

WILLIAM BYRD II (1674 — 1744) of Virginia was a major figure of Colonial America as both a public man and a writer. He wrote prolifically on many subjects, but his *Secret Diary and History of the Dividing Line,* not published until the 20[th]century, are among the most important works of American literature of the early 1700s. Below is his self-written epitaph for his tomb at Westover Plantation in Charles City County, Virginia.

Being born to one of the amplest fortunes in this country

he was early sent to England for his education

where under the care and direction of Sir Robert Southwell

and ever favored with his particular instructions

he made a happy proficiency in polite and varied learning.

By the means of the same noble friend

he was introduced to the acquaintance of many of the first

persons of the age

for knowledge, wit, virtue, birth, or high station

and particularly contracted a most intimate and bosom

friendship

with the learned and illustrious Charles Boyle, Earl of Orrery.

He was called to the Bar in the Middle Temple

studied for some time in the Low Countries,

visited the Court of France

and was chosen fellow of the Royal Society.

Thus eminently fitted for the service and ornament of his

country

he was made receiver general of his majesty's revenues here

was thrice pointed public agent to the court and ministry of

England

and being thirty-seven years a member

at last became President of the Council of the colony.

To all this were added a great elegance of taste and life
the wellbred gentleman and polite companion
the splendid economist and prudent father of a family
was the constant enemy of all exorbitant power
and hearty friend to the liberties of his country.

◆ ◆ ◆

UNKNOWN WRITER
(1781)

The Battle of King's Mountain

'Twas on a pleasant mountain
The Tory heathens lay,
With a doughty major at their head,
One Forguson, they say.

Cornwallis had detach'd him
A-thieving for to go,
And catch the Carolina men,
Or bring the rebels low.

The scamp had rang'd the country
In search of royal aid,
And with his owls, perched on high,
He taught them all his trade.

But ah! that fatal morning,
When Shelby brave drew near!
'T is certainly a warning
That ministers should hear.

And Campbell, and Cleveland,
And Colonel Sevier,
Each with a band of gallant men,
To Forguson appear.
Just as the sun was setting

Behind the western hills,
Just then our trusty rifles sent
A dose of leaden pills.

Up, up the steep together
Brave Williams led his troop,
And join'd by Winston, bold and true,
Disturb'd the Tory coop.

The royal slaves, the royal owls,
Flew high on every hand;
But soon they settled — gave a howl,
And quarter'd to Cleveland.

I would not tell the number
Of Tories slain that day,
But surely it is certain
That none did run away.

For all that were a-living,
Were happy to give up;
So let us make thanksgiving,
And pass the bright tin-cup.

To all the brave regiments,
Let's toast 'em for their health,
And may our good country
Have quietude and wealth.

◆ ◆ ◆

HENRY LEE (1756 — 1818), was an outstanding cavalry officer in the War of American Independence, Governor of Virginia, and father of Robert E. Lee. This is a part of his eulogy for his comrade Washington.

Henry Lee on George Washington

First in war, first in peace, and first in the hearts of his countrymen. He was second to none in the humble and endearing scenes of private life; pious, just, humane, temperate and sincere; uniform, dignified and commanding, his example was as edifying to all around him, as were the effects of that example lasting.

♦ ♦ ♦

THOMAS JEFFERSON (1732 — 1826) Here is Jefferson's self-composed epitaph. Note he does not consider the high offices he held in the U.S. federal government as his most important achievements.

Here was buried THOMAS JEFFERSON, Author of the Declaration of American Independence, of the Statute of Virginia for Religious Freedom, and Father of the University of Virginia

Born April 2, 1743 O. S.

Died July 4, 1826

♦ ♦ ♦

DOLLEY PAYNE MADISON (1768 — 1849) was the wife of President James Madison.

Lafayette

Born, nurtured, wedded, prized, within the pale
Of peers and princes, high in camp—at court—
He hears, in joyous youth, a wild report,
Swelling the murmurs of the Western gale,
Of a young people struggling to be free!
 Straight quitting all, across the wave he flies,
 Aids with his sword, wealth, blood, the high emprise!
And shares the glories of its victory,
 Then comes for fifty years a high romance
Of toils, reverses, sufferings, in the cause
 Of man and justice, liberty and France,
Crowned, at the last, with hope and wide applause.
 Champion of Freedom! Well thy race was run!
 All time shall hail thee, Europe's noblest Son!

♦ ♦ ♦

JOHN CHARLES McNEILL (1874 — 1907) was Poet Laureate of North Carolina whose work will appear later in this series. He wrote this verse in honour of the naval hero of the American Revolution John Paul Jones, whose first American home was North Carolina. Jones died in Paris in 1792. McNeill probably wrote about 1906 when Jones's presumed body was brought back for burial at Annapolis.

John Paul Jones

A century of silent suns

Have set since he was laid on sleep,

And now they bear with booming guns

And streaming banners o'er the deep

A withered skin and clammy hair

Upon a frame of human bones:

Whose corse? We neither know nor care,

Content to name it John Paul Jones.

His dust were as another's dust;

His bones—what boots it where they lie?

What matter where his sword is rust,

Or where, now dark, his eagle eye?

No foe need fear his arm again,

Nor love, nor praise can make him whole;

But o'er the farthest sons of men

Will brood the glory of his soul.

Careless though cenotaph or tomb

Shall tower his country's monument,

Let banners float and cannon boom,

A million-throated shout be spent,

Until his widowed sea shall laugh

With sunlight in her mantling foam,
While, to his tomb or cenotaph,
We bid our hero welcome home.

Twice exiled, let his ashes rest
At home, afar, or in the wave,
But keep his great heart with us, lest
Our nation's greatness find its grave;
And, while the vast deep listens by,
When armored wrong makes terms to right,
Keep on our lips his proud reply,
"Sir, I have but begun to fight!"

♦ ♦ ♦

THE SOUTH CAROLINA HYMN
(1807)

The music and lyrics for this song exist in manuscript form. It is apparently a response to the British outrage against the American navy in the *Chesapeake/Leopard* affair, an affair which led to the War of 1812 and to John C. Calhoun's entry into national politics. The song is thought to have been used at public events during the antebellum period.

Columbia's sons do greet the sound

That calls them to defend her rights.

The dauntless heart scorns ev'ry wound,

Who in the cause of freedom fights.

Brothers arise, our country calls.

The trumpet sound no heart appalls.

Our rights maintaining with our breath,

We'll fight for liberty or death.

♦ ♦ ♦

CHARLES COTESWORTH PINCKNEY (1749 — 1825) of South Carolina was one of the most outstanding figures of the American War of Independence and the early national period. This is his memorial tablet in St. Michael's Church, Charleston.

To the memory of

General Charles Cotesworth Pinckney

one of the founders of

the American Republic.

In war

he was the companion in arms

and the friend of Washington.

In peace

he enjoyed his unchanging confidence

and maintained with enlightened zeal

the principles of his administration

and of the Constitution.

As a Statesman

he bequeathed to his country the sentiment,

Millions for defence

not a cent for tribute.

As a lawyer,

his learning was various and profound

his principles pure, his practice liberal.

With all the accomplishments

of the gentleman

he combined the virtues of the patriot

And the piety of the Christian.

His name
is recorded in the history of his country
inscribed on the charter of her liberties,
And cherished in the affections of her citizens.
Obiit XVI August MDCCCXXV

♦ ♦ ♦

FRANCIS SCOTT KEY (1779 — 1843) of Maryland. The story is well known how Key composed "The Star-Spangled Banner" after he witnessed the repulse of the British attack on Fort McHenry in Baltimore harbour in 1814. It casts an interesting light on the official U.S. national anthem when one notes that Key's grandson, Frank Key Howard, was one of the first persons seized and imprisoned by Lincoln in his illegal armed occupation of Maryland, and that all of Key's kinfolks were Southern sympathizers, several serving in the Confederate Army. Like so much other Southern property, the anthem was confiscated for use of the Union in the War. Key's first selection refers to the Barbary War, in which the hero was Stephen Decatur, a Marylander. Some of Key's other verse may surprise readers who know only "The Star Spangled Banner."

Song

When the warrior returns, from the battle afar,

To the home and the country he nobly defended,

O! warm be the welcome to gladden his ear

And loud be the joy that his perils are ended.

In the full tide of song let his fame roll along.

To the feast-flowing board let us gratefully throng,

Where, mixed with the olive, the laurel shall wave,

And form a bright wreath for the brows of the brave.

Columbians! A band of your brothers behold,

Who claim the reward of your heart's warm emotion,

When your cause, when your honour, urged onward the bold.

In vain frowned the desert, in vain raged the ocean;

To a far distant shore, to the battle's wild roar,

They rushed, your fair fame and your rights to secure:

Then, mixed with the olive, the laurel shall wave.

And form a bright wreath for the brows of the brave.

In the conflict resistless, each toil they endured,
'Till their foes fled dismayed from the war's desolation.
And pale beamed the Crescent, its splendor obscured
By the light of the star spangled flag of our nation.
Where each radiant star gleamed a meteor of war.
And the turbaned heads bowed to its terrible glare.
Now, mixed with the olive, the laurel shall wave,
And form a bright wreath for the brows of the brave.

Our fathers, who stand on the summit of fame,
Shall exultingly hear of their sons the proud story:
How their young bosoms glow'd with the patriotic flame,
How they fought, how they fell, in the blaze of their glory.
How triumphant they rode o'er the towering flood,
And stained the blue waters with infidel blood;
How, mixed with the olive, the laurel did wave,
And formed a bright wreath for the brows of the brave.

Then welcome the warrior returned from afar
To the home and the country he nobly defended:
Let the thanks due to valour now gladden his ear,
And loud be the joy that his perils are ended.
In the full tide of song let his flame roll along,
To the feast-flowing board let us gratefully throng,
Where, mixed with the olive, the laurel shall wave,
And form a bright wreath for the brows of the brave.

♦

The Star - Spangled Banner

Oh, say, can you see, by the dawn's early light,
What so proudly we hailed at the twilight's last gleaming?
Whose broad stripes and bright stars, thru the perilous fight,
O'er the ramparts we watched, were so gallantly streaming?
And the rockets' red glare, the bombs bursting in air,
Gave proof thro' the night that our flag was still there.
Oh, say, does that star-spangled banner yet wave
O'er the land of the free and the home of the brave?

On the shore dimly seen thro' the mists of the deep,
Where the foe's haughty host in dread silence reposes,
What is that which the breeze, o'er the towering steep,
As it fitfully blows, half conceals, half discloses?
Now it catches the gleam of the morning's first beam,
In full glory reflected, now shines on the stream.
Tis the star-spangled banner; oh, long may it wave
O'er the land of the free and the home of the brave!

And where is that band who so vauntingly swore
That the havoc of war and the battle's confusion
A home and a country should leave us no more?
Their blood has washed out their foul footsteps' pollution.
No refuge could save the hireling and slave
From the terror of flight, or the gloom of the grave:
And the star-spangled banner in triumph doth wave
O'er the land of the free and the home of the brave.

Oh, thus be it ever when freemen shall stand,
Between their loved homes and the war's desolation;
Blest with victory and peace, may the heav'n-rescued land
Praise the Power that hath made and preserved us a nation!
Then conquer we must, when our cause. it is just,
And this be our motto: "In God is our trust!"
And the star-spangled banner in triumph shall wave
O'er the land of the free and the home of the brave!

♦

Before the Lord We Bow

Before the Lord we bow, the God who reigns above,
And rules the world below, boundless in power and love.
Our thanks we bring in joy and praise, our hearts we raise
To Heaven's high King.

The nation Thou has blest may well Thy love declare,
From foes and fears at rest, protected by Thy care.
For this fair land, for this bright day, our thanks we pay,
Gifts of Thy hand.

May every mountain height, each vale and forest green,
Shine in Thy Word's pure light, and its rich fruits be seen!
May every tongue be turned to praise, and join to raise
A grateful song.

Earth, here thy Maker's voice, thy great Redeemer own;
Believe, obey, rejoice, and worship Him alone.
Cast down thy pride, thy sin deplore and bow before
The Crucified.
And when in Power he comes, O may our native land,
From all its rending tombs, send forth a glorious band.
A countless throng, ever to sing Heaven's high King
Salvation's song.

♦ ♦ ♦

WASHINGTON ALLSTON (1779 — 1843) of South Carolina was one of the most important of early American painters. The first two poems were written in response to his viewing of major artistic works in Italy.

*On a Falling Group in the Last Judgment
of Michael Angelo, in the Cappella Sistina*

How vast how dread, o'erwhelming, is the thought

Of space interminable! to the soul

A circling weight that crushes into naught

Her mighty faculties! a wondrous whole,

Without or parts, beginning, or an end!

How fearful, then, on desperate wings to send

The fancy e'en amid the waste profound!

Yet, born as if all daring to astound,

Thy giant hand, O Angelo, hath hurled

E'en human forms, with all their mortal weight,

Down the dread void,—fall endless as their fate!

Already now they seem from world to world

For ages thrown; yet doomed, another past,

Another still to reach, nor e'er to reach the last!

♦

*On the Group of the Three Angels before
the Tent of Abraham, by Raffaelle, in the Vatican*

O, now I feel as though another sense,

From heaven descending, had informed my

soul; I feel the pleasurable, full control

In thee, celestial Group, embodied lives

The subtile mystery, that speaking gives

Itself resolved; the essences combined
Of Motion ceaseless, Unity complete.
Borne like a leaf by some soft eddying wind,
Mine eyes, impelled as by enchantment sweet,
From part to part with circling motion rove,
Yet seem unconscious of the power to move;
From line to line through endless changes run,
O'er countless shapes, yet seem to gaze on One.

♦

The French Revolution

The Earth has had her visitation. Like to this
She hath not known, save when the mounting waters
Made of her orb one universal ocean.
For now the Tree that grew in Paradise,
The deadly Tree that first gave Evil motion,
And sent its poison through Earth's sons and daughters,
Had struck again its root in every land;
And now its fruit was ripe,—about to fall,—
And now a mighty Kingdom raised the hand,
To pluck and eat. Then from his throne stepped forth
The King of Hell, and stood upon the Earth:
But not, as once, upon the Earth to crawl.
A Nation's congregated form he took,
Till, drunk with sin and blood, Earth to her centre shook.

♦ ♦ ♦

RICHARD HENRY WILDE (1789 — 1847) of Georgia gave up a successful career as lawyer and Congressman to pursue the Muse in Europe. This poem, though perhaps out of fashion, was praised by Byron and was long immensely popular in the English-speaking world. The Yankee black-face minstrel show impresario Stephen Foster "appropriated" some of the lines and set them to music under a different title.

My Life is Like the Summer Rose

My life is like the summer rose.

That opens to the morning sky.

But, ere the shades of evening close,

Is scattered on the ground—to die!

Yet on the rose's humble bed

The sweetest dews of night are shed.

As if she wept the waste to see—

But none shall weep a tear for me!

My life is like the autumn leaf

That trembles in the moon's pale ray:

Its hold is frail—its date is brief.

Restless—and soon to pass away!

Yet, ere that leaf shall fall and fade.

The parent tree will mourn its shade,

The winds bewail the leafless tree—

But none shall breathe a sigh for me!

My life is like the prints, which feet

Have left on Tampa's desert strand;

Soon as the rising tide shall beat.

All trace will vanish from the stand:

Yet, as if grieving to efface

All vestige of the human race.
On that lone shore loud moans the sea—
But none, alas! Shall mourn for me!

♦

A Farewell to America
FAREWELL, my more than fatherland!
Home of my heart and friends, adieu!
Lingering beside some foreign strand,
How oft shall I remember you!
How often, o'er the waters blue,
Send back a sign to those I leave,
The loving and beloved few,
Who grieve for me,—for whom I grieve!

We part!—no matter how we part,
There are some thoughts we utter not,
Deep treasured in our inmost heart,
Never revealed, and ne'er forgot!
Why murmur at the common lot?
We part!—I speak not of the pain,—
But when shall I each lovely spot
And each loved face behold again?

It must be months,—it may be years,—
It may—but no!—I will not fill
Fond hearts with gloom,—fond eyes with tears,
"Curious to shape uncertain ill."
Though humble,—few and far,—yet, still
Those hearts and eyes are ever dear;

Theirs is the love no time can chill,
The truth no chance or change can sear!

All I have seen, and all I see,
Only endears them more and more;
Friends cool, hopes fade, and hours flee,
Affection lives when all is o'er!
Farewell, my more than native shore!
I do not seek or hope to find,
Roam where I will, what I deplore
To leave with them and thee behind!

♦

To the Mocking-Bird

Winged mimic of the woods! thou motley fool!
Who shall thy gay buffoonery describe?
Thine ever-ready notes of ridicule
Pursue thy fellows still with jest and gibe.
Wit, sophist, songster, Yorick of thy tribe,
Thou sportive satirist of Nature's school,
To thee the palm of scoffing we ascribe.
Arch-mocker and mad Abbot of Misrule!
For such thou art by day—but all night long
Thou pourest a soft, sweet, pensive, solemn strain,
As if thou didst in this thy moonlight song
Like to the melancholy Jacques complain,
Musing on falsehood, folly, vice, and wrong,
And sighing for thy motley coat again.

♦ ♦ ♦

EDWARD COOTE PINKNEY (1802 — 1828) of Maryland was born and partly raised in England where his father, William Pinkney, was the U.S. Minister. After publishing a good deal of poetry, he attempted to join the Mexican Navy during that country's war of independence. From this venture Pinkney returned home to Baltimore, his health shattered. He continued to write prolifically well-regarded verse until his death at 27. Pinkney's grave is located near Sidney Lanier's in Baltimore.

The Indian's Bride

I

Why is that graceful female here

With yon red hunter of the deer?

Of gentle mien and shape, she seems

For civil halls designed,

Yet with the stately savage walks

As she were of his kind.

Look on her leafy diadem,

Enriched with many a floral gem:

Those simple ornaments about

Her candid brow, disclose

The loitering Spring's last violet,

And Summer's earliest rose;

But not a flower lies breathing there,

Sweet as herself, or half so fair.

Exchanging lustre with the sun,

A part of day she strays—

A glancing, living, human smile,

On nature's face she plays.

Can none instruct me what are these

Companions of the lofty trees?—

II

Intent to blend with his her lot,
Fate formed her all that he was not;
And, as by mere unlikeness thoughts
Associate we see,
Their hearts from very difference caught
A perfect sympathy.
The household goddess here to be
Of that one dusky votary—
She left her pallid countrymen,
An earthling most divine.
And sought in this sequestered wood
A solitary shrine.
Behold them roaming hand in hand,
Like night and sleep, along the land;
Observe their movements:—he for her
Restrains his active stride,
While she assumes a bolder gait
To ramble at his side:
Thus, even as the steps they frame,
Their souls fast alter to the same.
The one forsakes ferocity,
And momently grows mild;
The other tempers more and more
The artful with the wild.
She humanizes him, and he
Educates her to liberty.

III

Oh, say not they must soon be old,
Their limbs prove faint, their breasts feel cold!
Yet envy I that sylvan pair,
More than my words express,
The singular beauty of their lot,
And seeming happiness.
They have not been reduced to share
The painful pleasures of despair:
Their sun declines not in the sky,
Nor are their wishes cast,
Like shadows of the afternoon,
Repining towards the past:
With naught to dread, or to repent,
The present yields them full content.
In solitude there is no crime;
Their actions are all free,
And passion lends their way of life
The only dignity;
And how should they have any cares
Whose interest contends with theirs?—

IV

The world, or all they know of it,
Is theirs:—for them the stars are lit;
For them the earth beneath is green,
The heavens above are bright;
For them the moon doth wax and wane,

And decorate the night;
For them the branches of those trees
Wave musick in the vernal breeze;
For them upon that dancing spray
The free bird sits and sings,
And glitt'ring insects flit about
Upon delighted wings;
For them that brook, the brakes among,
Murmurs its small and drowsy song;
For them the many coloured clouds
Their shapes diversify,
And change at once, like smiles and frowns,
Th' expression of the sky.
For them, and by them, all is gay,
And fresh and beautiful as they:
The images their minds receive,
Their minds assimilate,
To outward forms imparting thus
The glory of their state.
Could aught be painted otherwise
Than fair, seen through her star-bright eyes?
He too, because she fills his sight,
Each object falsely sees;
The pleasure that he has in her,
Makes all things seem to please.
And this is love;—and it is life
They lead, that Indian and his wife.

♦ ♦ ♦

THE ALAMO

Last Message from the Alamo

Commandancy of the Alamo, Bexar, Feb. 24,1836

FELLOW-CITIZENS AND COMPATRIOTS: I am besieged by a thousand or more of the Mexicans under Santa Anna. I have sustained a continued bombardment for twenty-four hours, and have not lost a man. The enemy have demanded a surrender at discretion; otherwise the garrison is to be put to the sword, if the place is taken. I have answered the summons with a cannon-shot, and our flag still waves proudly from the walls. I shall never surrender or retreat. Then I call on you in the name of liberty, of patriotism, and of everything dear to the American character to come to our aid with all dispatch. The enemy are receiving reinforcements daily, and will no doubt increase to three or four thousand in four or five days. Though this call may be neglected, I am determined to sustain myself as long as possible, and die like a soldier who never forgets what is due to his own honour and that of his country. Victory or death!

W. Barrett Travis, Lieutenant-Colonel Commanding

◆

Original Memorial Inscription at the Alamo

To the God of the Fearless and Free is dedicated this Altar made from the Ruins of the Alamo.

Thermopylae had her Messenger of Defeat, but the Alamo had none.

Be they enrolled with Leonidas in the Host of the Mighty Dead.

Blood of Heroes hath stained me, let the Stones of the Alamo speak that their Immolation be not forgotten.

◆

Stark Young (1881 — 1963) of Mississippi is best known as one of the Twelve Southerners of the manifesto *I'll Take My Stand*, and for his novel *So Red the Rose*. He wrote this tribute to Southern history early in his career.

The Alamo

Is then Thermopylae come from the shade

Of ancient death and grand oblivion?

Ere dawn they charge. Stand, little garrison!

On, fail not God and Texas! They have made

The wall—hold then your church and carronade.

The loop-holes flame, the aqueducts will run

Crimson with blood—ye fight a score with one.

The smoke dies down, your glory cannot fade.

The rising sun finds death and silence there.

Beside the wall Travis lies slain, and nigh

The chapel glorious Crockett, fallen among

The hostile carnage and our few. Hear,

O Mexico! This is no victory,

For from these veins are wells of freedom sprung!

♦ ♦ ♦

II. Flourishing

EDGAR ALLAN POE (1809 — 1849) of Virginia was the great creative genius of 19th century American literature in poetry, fiction, and criticism. Although accidentally born in Boston and spending part of his foreshortened life earning a living in New York, Poe was, and unequivocally considered himself to be, a Southerner. In all his career he was in combat with the New England literary establishment, which he openly ridiculed as "the Frog-pondians," croaking writers who imagined that their little empire in Boston was the center of the world. While the celebrated authors of New England were writing ditties about "barefoot boys with cheeks of tan," sleigh rides to grandma's house, and an imaginary Indian named Hiawatha, not to mention Emerson's conceited secular sermons, Poe was expanding the musical potential of the English language and the frontiers of human imagination. The great Irish poet William Butler Yeats wrote that Poe was "certainly the greatest of American poets, and always and for every land, a great lyric poet." Like some other Southern writers, notably Faulkner, Poe's genius was appreciated in Europe when his reputation was ignored or slandered in Northeastern literary circles. It is possible to give only a slight but hopefully suggestive sample from his large body of poetic work.

Alone

From childhood's hour I have not been

As others were — I have not seen

As others saw — I could not bring

My passions from a common spring —

From the same source I have not taken

My sorrow — I could not awaken

My heart to joy at the same tone —

And all I lov'd — I lov'd alone —

Then— in my childhood — in the dawn

Of a most stormy life — was drawn

From ev'ry depth of good and ill

The mystery which binds me still —

From the torrent, or the fountain —

From the red cliff of the mountain —
From the sun that 'round me roll'd
In its autumn tint of gold —
From the lightning in the sky
As it pass'd me flying by —
From the thunder, and the storm —
And the cloud that took the form
(When the rest of Heaven was blue)
Of a demon in my view —

♦

Israfel

In Heaven a spirit doth dwell
"Whose heart-strings are a lute;"
None sing so wildly well
As the angel Israfel,
And the giddy stars (so legends tell),
Ceasing their hymns, attend the spell
Of his voice, all mute.

Tottering above
In her highest noon,
The enamored moon
Blushes with love,
While, to listen, the red levin
(With the rapid Pleiads, even,
Which were seven,)
Pauses in Heaven.

And they say (the starry choir
And the other listening things)
That Israfeli's fire
Is owing to that lyre
By which he sits and sings—
The trembling living wire
Of those unusual strings.

But the skies that angel trod,
Where deep thoughts are a duty—
Where Love's a grown-up God—
Where the Houri glances are Imbued
with all the beauty
Which we worship in a star.
Therefore thou art not wrong,
Israfeli, who despisest
An unimpassioned song;
To thee the laurels belong,
Best bard, because the wisest!
Merrily live, and long!

The ecstasies above
With thy burning measures suit—
Thy grief, thy joy, thy hate, thy love,
With the fervor of thy lute—
Well may the stars be mute!

Yes, Heaven is thine; but this
Is a world of sweets and sours;

Our flowers are merely — flowers,

And the shadow of thy perfect bliss Is

the sunshine of ours.

If l could dwell

Where Israfel

Hath dwelt, and he where I,

He might not sing so wildly well

A mortal melody,

While a bolder note than this might swell

From my lyre within the sky.

◆

To Marie Louise

Not long ago, the writer of these lines,

In the mad pride of intellectuality,

Maintained "the Power of Words"—denied that ever

A thought arose within the human brain

Beyond the utterance of the human tongue:

And now, as if in mockery of that boast,

Two words—two foreign soft dissyllables—

Two gentle sounds made only to be murmured

By angels dreaming in the moon-lit "dew

That hands like chains of pearl on Hermon hill"

Have stirred from out the abysses of his heart

Unthought-like thoughts—scarcely the shades of thought—

Bewildering fantasies—far richer visions

Than even seraph harper, Israfel,

Who "had the sweetest voice of all God's creatures,"

Would hope to utter. Ah, Marie Louise!
In deep humility I own that now
All pride—all thought of power—all hope of fame—
All wish for Heaven—is merged forevermore
Beneath the palpitating tide of passion
Heaped o'er my soul by thee. Its spells are broken—
The pen falls powerless from my shivering hand—
With that dear name as text I cannot write—
I cannot speak—I cannot even think—
Alas! I cannot feel; for 'tis not feeling—
This standing motionless upon the golden
Threshold of the wide-open gate of Dreams,
Gazing, entranced, adown the gorgeous vista,
And thrilling as I see upon the right—
Upon the left—and all the way along,
Amid the clouds of glory, far away
To where the prospect terminates—thee only.

◆

Sonnet — To Science

Science! true daughter of Old Time thou art!
    Who alterest all things with thy peering eyes.
Why preyest thou thus upon the poet's heart,
    Vulture, whose wings are dull realities?
How should he love thee? or how deem thee wise,
    Who wouldst not leave him in his wandering
To seek for treasure in the jewelled skies,
    Albeit he soared with an undaunted wing?
Hast thou not dragged Diana from her car,
    And driven the Hamadryad from the wood

To seek a shelter in some happier star?
    Hast thou not torn the Naiad from her flood,
The Elfin from the green grass, and from me
The summer dream beneath the tamarind tree?

◆

Annabel Lee

It was many and many a year ago,
    In a kingdom by the sea,
That a maiden there lived whom you may know
    By the name of Annabel Lee;
And this maiden she lived with no other thought
    Than to love and be loved by me.

I was a child and she was a child,
    In this kingdom by the sea,
But we loved with a love that was more than love—
    I and my Annabel Lee—
With a love that the wingèd seraphs of Heaven
    Coveted her and me.

And this was the reason that, long ago,
    In this kingdom by the sea,
A wind blew out of a cloud, chilling
    My beautiful Annabel Lee;
So that her highborn kinsmen came
    And bore her away from me,
To shut her up in a sepulchre
    In this kingdom by the sea.

The angels, not half so happy in Heaven,
    Went envying her and me—
Yes!—that was the reason (as all men know,
    In this kingdom by the sea)
That the wind came out of the cloud by night,
    Chilling and killing my Annabel Lee.

But our love it was stronger by far than the love
    Of those who were older than we—
Of many far wiser than we—
    And neither the angels in Heaven above
Nor the demons down under the sea
    Can ever dissever my soul from the soul
Of the beautiful Annabel Lee;

For the moon never beams, without bringing me dreams
    Of the beautiful Annabel Lee;
And the stars never rise, but I feel the bright eyes
    Of the beautiful Annabel Lee;
And so, all the night-tide, I lie down by the side
    Of my darling—my darling—my life and my bride,
In her sepulchre there by the sea—
    In her tomb by the sounding sea.

◆

Eldorado

Gaily bedight,
A gallant knight,
In sunshine and in shadow,
Had journeyed long,
Singing a song,
In search of Eldorado.

But he grew old—
This knight so bold—
And o'er his heart a shadow—
Fell as he found
No spot of ground
That looked like Eldorado.

And, as his strength
Failed him at length,
He met a pilgrim shadow—
'Shadow,' said he,
'Where can it be—
This land of Eldorado?'

Over the Mountains
Of the Moon,
Down the Valley of the Shadow,
Ride, boldly ride,'
The shade replied,—
'If you seek for Eldorado!'

♦ ♦ ♦

WILLIAM ALEXANDER CARUTHERS (1802 — 1846) of Virginia is best known for his novel *The Knights of the Golden Horseshoe*, published in 1835. This verse is taken from that book and reflects some thoughts of the half of Virginia-born people, black and white, who were moving south and west at the time.

Negro Song

"Farewell, Old Beginny,

I lebe you now maybe forebber;

I'm gwine to lebe de Chesapeake,

I lebe you crab, you prawn, you oyster—

Way down in Old Beginny."

"My fishing-smack, my net and tackle,

I lebe you by the ribber side;

I gwine to lebe de swamp and woods,

Where de coon and possum sleep—

Way down in Old Beginny."

"All my friends I lebe behind me—

Ben, Harry, Bill, and old Aunt Dinah,

Maum, Mary, and de Sarah child,

And my young misses, I 'blige to lebe you—

Way down in Old Beginny."

"De rattle-snake, de deer, de turkey,

He got dis country all to eself—

He high like steeple, and deep like well,

No like de shore I lebe behind me—

Way down in Old Beginny."

"A long farewell, my Old Beginny;
I gwine fight cussed Injun now;
He sculp old June, he broke he banjo,
He no more sing to he young missus—
Way down in Old Beginny."

"The chimbly-corner's all dark now,
No banjo da to make him merry;
A long farewell to my old missus—
A long farewell to my old missus—
Way down in Old Beginny."

◆ ◆ ◆

MIRABEAU BUONAPARTE LAMAR (1798 — 1859) of Texas moved from his native Georgia to the Texas Republic in 1835. He took a conspicuous part in the Texas War of Independence and was cited by Sam Houston for outstanding bravery at the Battle of San Jacinto. Lamar served in the Texas government and followed Houston as President. He was also a prolific poet. His verses were often addressed to or about ladies—his mother, sister, daughter, or others he admired. His work gives something of a hint of the mind of the early Southern settlers of Texas.

The Daughter of Mendoza

O lend to me, sweet nightingale,
 Your music by the fountains,
And lend to me your cadences,
 O river of the mountains!
That I may sing my gay brunette,
A diamond spark in coral set,
Gem for a prince's coronet—
 The daughter of Mendoza.

How brilliant is the morning star!
 The evening star, how tender!
The light of both is in her eye,
 Their softness and their splendor.
But for the lash that shades their light
They were too dazzling for the sight;
And when she shuts them, all is night—
 The daughter of Mendoza.

O! ever bright and beauteous one,
 Bewildering and beguiling,
The lute is in thy silvery tones,

The rainbow in thy smiling.
And thine is, too, o'er hill and dell,
The bounding of the young gazelle,
The arrow's flight and ocean's swell—
Sweet daughter of Mendoza!

What though, perchance, we meet no more—
What though too soon we sever?
Thy form will float like emerald light,
Before my vision ever.
For who can see and then forget
The glories of my gay brunette?
Thou art too bright a star to set—
Sweet daughter of Mendoza!

♦

Oh, Do Not Ask Me Now For Rhyme
To My Daughter, Rebecca Ann

OH, do not ask me now for rhyme,
For I am lonely-hearted;
And lost are all the dear delights
The Muses once imparted.
I sigh no more for Hybla's dews,
Nor Helicon's bright water;
I only crave a sable wave
Of Lethe's stream, my Daughter.

And wouldst thou share thy father's woes,
Partake his bitter weeping?

Then seek with him yon valley's shade,
Where beauty's wreck is sleeping;
For in that dark and lonely place —
Death's solemn, silent quarter —
Was laid the pride of all her sex,
The mother of my Daughter.

She was all bright and beautiful,
A floating star before me,
Whose lustre was my guiding light,
For ever shining o'er me;
So much of heaven in all her ways,
How often have I thought her
Some angel sent us from the skies,
To bless this earth, my Daughter!

It was from her alone I drew
My minstrel inspiration;
But when she died and left me here —
My soul in desolation —
I broke the shell she loved so well,
Destroyed the songs I wrought her;
Nor can my voice again rejoice
In cheerful strains, my Daughter.

Then name some other boon, my child; —
Thou know'st I can deny thee
No gift thine innocence demands,
While thou art smiling by me:

But should I dare re-string the harp
By Chattahoochee's water,
The bitter tears of other years
Would flow afresh, my Daughter.

♦

Soldier of the Cross
Inscribed to the Pioneer Preacher of Texas.

NAY — tell me not of dangers dire
That lie in duty's path;
A Warrior of the Cross can feel
No fear of human wrath.
Where'er the Prince of Darkness holds
His earthly reign abhorred,
Sword of the Spirit! thee I draw,
And battle for the Lord.

I go, I go to break the chains
That bind the erring mind,
And give the freedom that I feel,
To all of human kind;
But oh, I wear no burnished steel,
And seek no gory field;
My weapon is the Word of God,
His promise is my shield.

And thus equipped, why need I fear,
Though hosts around me rise? —
There is a power in gospel truth

No heathen can despise;
And he who boldly fights with that,
Will through more perils wade
Than the vain warrior, trusting to
His bright Damascus blade.

No blasts by land or sea can shake
The purpose of my soul;
The tempest of a thousand winds
May sweep from pole to pole,
Yet still serene, and fixed in faith,
All fear of death I scorn —
I know it is my Father's work —
He's with me in the storm.

Then let me go where duty calls,
Where God himself commands —
Bearing the banner of his Son
To dark and distant lands;
And if the high and holy cause
Require my early fall,
A recreant he who would not die
For Him who died for all.

*Written at the suggestion of Mrs. Dr. Hoxey,
Independence, Washington County, Texas.*

♦

Apology

I NEVER hoped in life to claim
A passport to exalted fame;
'T is not for this I sometimes frame
The simple song —
Contented still, with humble name,
To move along.

I write because there's joy in rhyme;
It cheers an evening's idle time;
And though my verse the true sublime
May never reach,
Yet Heaven will never call it crime,
If truth it teach.

The labour steals the heart from wo;
It makes it oft with rapture glow;
And always teaches to forego
Each low desire;
Then why on those our blame bestow
Who strike the lyre?

If virtue in the song be blent,
I know no reason to repent
My hours of studious content,
And lettered joy;
'T were well if leisure ne'er was spent
In worse employ.

♦

Arm For The Southern Land

(1833)
Inscribed To My Nephew, Lucius M. Lamar
(Tune — "Oft In The Stilly Night")

ARM for the Southern land,

All fear of death disdaining;

Low lay the tyrant hand

Our sacred rights profaning!

Each hero draws

In Freedom's cause,

And meets the foe with bravery;

The servile race,

And tory base,

May safety seek in slavery.

Chains for the dastard knave—

Recreant limbs should wear them;

But blessings on the brave

Whose valor will not bear them!

Stand by your injured State,

And let no feuds divide you;

On tyrants pour your hate,

And common vengeance guide you.

Our foes should feel

Proud freemen's steel,

For freemen's rights contending;

Where'er they die,

There let them lie,

To dust in scorn descending.

Thus may each traitor fall,
Who dare as foe invade us;
Eternal fame to all
Who shall in battle aid us!

Proud land! shall she invoke
Another's hand to right her?—
No!—her own avenging stroke
Shall backward roll the smiter.
Ye tyrant band,
With ropes of sand,
Go bind the rushing river;
More weak and vain
Is slavery's chain,
While GOD is freedom's giver.
Then welcome to the day
We meet the proud oppressor,
For GOD will be our stay—
Our right hand and redressor.

Columbus, Georgia, 1833

♦

Carmelita
Monterey, Mexico

O Carmelita, know ye not
For whom all hearts are pining?
And know ye not, in Beauty's sky,
The brightest planet shining?
Then learn it now—for thou art she,
Thy nation's jewel, born to be
By all beloved, but most by me—
O DONNA CARMELITA!

But wo is me thy love to lose,
Apart from thee abiding;
Between us roars a gloomy stream,
Our destiny dividing.
That stream with blood incarnadined,
Flows from thy nation's erring mind,
And rolls with ruin to thy kind,
O DONNA CARMELITA!

'Tis mine, while floating on the tide,
To stick to love and duty;
I draw my sabre on the foe,
I strike my harp to beauty;
And who shall say the soldier's wrong,
Who, while he battles with the strong,
Still softens war with gentle song,
O DONNA CARMELITA?

I soon shall seek the battle-field,
Where Freedom's flag is waving—
My Texas comrades by my side,
All perils madly braving;
I only grieve to think each blow,
That vengeance bids the steel bestow,
Must make thee mine eternal foe,
O DONNA CARMELITA!

Full well I know thy pride will spurn
The brightest wreaths I bring thee;
Full well I know thou wilt not heed
The sweetest songs I sing thee;
Yet, all despite thy scorn and hate,
Despite the thousand ills of fate,
I still my soul must dedicate—
To DONNA CARMELITA!

Then fare thee well, dear, lovely one—
May happiness attend thee;
Ten thousand harps exalt thy name,
Ten thousand swords defend thee:
And when the sod is on my breast,
My harp and sabre both at rest,
May thee and thine be greatly blest,
O DONNA CARMELITA!

♦

In Life's Unclouded, Gayer Hour
To A Lady In Houston, Texas

In life's unclouded, gayer hour,
I bowed to beauty's sway;
I felt the eye's despotic power,
And trembled in its ray;
But beauty now no more enthralls—
Its magic spell hath flown;
Upon my heart it coldly falls,
Like moonlight on a stone.

The chords of feeling soon were broke,
Where love delighted played;
Affliction dealt too rude a stroke,
And all in ruin laid;
Yet, lady fair, there was a time
I might have worshipped thee;
Thy beauty would have been the shrine
Of my idolatry.

That time is past, and I am left
A sad sojourner here—
Of hope, of joy, of all bereft,
That makes existence dear.
Despair hath o'er my bosom cast
The gloom of starless night—
A darkness which through life must last,
Unpierced by beauty's light.

♦ ♦ ♦

WILLIAM WALKER (1808 — 1875) of South Carolina. It would be hard to find any American who has played a more important role in Christian music than the Baptist layman "Singing Billy" Walker. In 1835 he published *Southern Harmony*, a shape-note hymnal with lyrics and music for over two hundred songs, more than one hundred of which were taken from the folk realm and had never been printed. He strenuously traveled the Southeastern States teaching shape-note singing schools in remote areas. *Southern Harmony* was the mainstay of musical worship in hundreds of rural churches for several generations. The book was expanded and republished in 1854. It is said to have sold an amazing 600,000 copies and is still available in various formats. Walker wrote a number of hymns of his own, but his most prolific work was as a collector and arranger, putting together in original and creative ways the lyrics and music which had reached America as unwritten folk literature. His most important work in this regard is "Amazing Grace." The words were written by the Englishman John Newton in 1772. Many failed attempts were made to set them to music. It was Walker who created the classical version we now know by uniting the words to the traditional music called "New Britain" which he had learned from his mother. (You will not be surprised to learn that PBS television did a multi-part series on "Amazing Grace" without mentioning William Walker even once.) Walker continued to travel extensively and went to Richmond to bring spiritual comfort to Confederate hospitals. His amazing and prolific work has penetrated American culture. Some of Walker's creations are so familiar that they have been described as "folk" songs. Many others are today in the hymnals of many denominations, usually without attribution. Here is one of Walker's own lyrics.

Louisiana

Come, little children, now we may

Partake a little morsel,

For little songs and little ways

Adorn'd a great apostle;

A little drop of Jesus' blood

Can make a feast of union;

It is by little steps we move

Into a full communion.

A little faith does mighty deeds,
Quite past all my recounting;
Faith, like a little mustard seed,
Can move a lofty mountain.
A little charity and zeal,
A little tribulation,
A little patience makes us feel
Great peace and consolation.

A little cross with cheerfulness,
A little self denial,
Will serve to make our troubles less
And bear the greatest trial.
The Spirit like a little dove
On Jesus once descended;
To show his meekness and his love
The emblem was intended.

The title of the little Lamb
Unto our Lord was given;
Such was our Savior's little name,
The Lord of earth and heaven.
A little voice that's small and still
Can rule the whole creation;
A little stone the earth shall fill,
And humble every nation.

A little zeal supplies the soul,
It doth the heart inspire;

A little spark lights up the whole,
And sets the crowd on fire.
A little union serves to hold
The good and tender hearted;
It's stronger than a chain of gold
And never can be parted.

Come, let us labor here below,
And who can be the straitest;
For in God's kingdom, all must know
The least shall be the greatest.
O give us, Lord, a little drop
Of heavenly love and union
O may we never, never stop
Short of full communion.

◆ ◆ ◆

SOUTHERN FOLK SONGS. Fiddle, guitar, and banjo were staples of Southern life and like most attributes of Southern life were carried westward by the people. American "folk" music traces to this source. The "folk" music played and created. drew upon old and loved tunes and ballads brought from the British Isles. The tunes were adapted and given Americanised or new lyrics. The music being living, it exhibited many local variations and spontaneous amendments, so that an exact origin is usually impossible to establish. This tradition of natural music continued well into the 20th century in gospel and in various expressions of Southern music which were misleadingly dubbed country and Western, bluegrass, and Western swing. The tradition, popularised by radio and recordings, boasted some of the greatest and most original composers, writers, and performers in American music. Though somewhat commercialised, Southern music maintained much of its rootedness, creativity and distinctive Southernness for a long time. In the 1990s or thereabouts, takeovers by foreign corporations and the advent of vulgar music videos transformed "country music," except for a few holdouts.

Handsome Mary, The Lily of the West

When first I came to Louisville some pleasure there to find,

A damsel fair from Lexington was pleasing my mind.

Her cherry cheeks and ruby lips, like arrows pierced my breast,—

They called her Handsome Mary, the Lily of the West.

I courted her awhile, in hopes her love to gain,

But she proved false to me which caused me much pain.

She robbed me of my liberty, deprived me of my rest,—

They called her Handsome Mary, the Lily of the West.

One evening as I rambled, down by a shady grove,

I saw a man of low degree conversing with my love.

They were singing songs of melody, while I was sore distressed,

O faithless, faithless Mary, the Lily of the West!

I stepped up to my rival, my dagger in my hand.
I caught him by the collar, and boldly bade him stand;
Being driven to desperation, I stabbed him in the breast,
But was betrayed by Mary, the Lily of the West!

At length the day of trial came, I boldly made my plea,
But the judge and jury they soon convicted me.
To deceive both judge and jury so modestly she dressed,
And there she swore my life away, the Lily of the West.

◆

Shenandoah is the beautiful river valley of Virginia. According to some authorities the song originated among river boatman and fur trappers of the upper Missouri River valley and Shenandoah was an Indian chief whose daughter was beloved. It is hardly credible that there is no connection to Virginia, especially since many of the men who first penetrated the northern plains and mountains were Virginians and other Southerners.

Shenandoah

Oh, Shenandoah,

I long to see you,

Away you rolling river.

Oh Shenandoah,

I long to see you,

Away, I'm bound away,

'cross the wide Missouri.

Oh Shenandoah,

I love your daughter,

Away, you rolling river.

For her I'd cross,

Your roaming waters,

Away, I'm bound away,

'Cross the wide Missouri.

'Tis seven years,

since last I've seen you,

And hear your rolling river.

'Tis seven years,

since last I've seen you,

Away, we're bound away,
Across the wide Missouri.

Oh Shenandoah,
I long to see you,
And hear your rollin river.
Oh Shenandoah,
I long to see you,
Away, we're bound away,
Across the wide Missouri.

♦

Katy Wells

You ask what makes this darky sad,
　　Why he like others am not gay,
What makes the tear flow down his cheek
　　From early morn till close of day?
My story, darkies, you shall hear
　　For in my memory fresh it dwells,
'Twill cause you all to drop a tear
　　On the grave of my sweet Katy Wells.

CHORUS:
When the birds were singing in the morning,
　　And the myrtle and the ivy were in bloom
When the sun o'er the hills was dawning;
　　'Twas then we laid her in the tomb.

Oh, I remember well the day
    When we together roamed the dells,
I kissed her cheek and named the day
    When I should marry Katy Wells,
But death came in my cabin door,
    And stole from me my joy and pride,
And when I found she was no more,
    I laid my banjo down and cried.
The springtime has no charms for me,
    The flowers that bloom around the dells
There's a form I long to see;
    The form of my sweet Katy Wells.
Chorus—

I've sometimes wished that I was dead,
    And laid beside her in the tomb,
For sorrow now bows down my head
    In silence to the midnight gloom,
I'm longing for the day to come
    When I shall clasp her to my heart,
While in the heavenly fields we roam
    And never, never more to part.
Chorus—

♦ ♦ ♦

STEPHEN COLLINS FOSTER (1826 — 1864) was a Northerner, born in Pennsylvania. He is said to be the best known and most popular musical figure in 19th century America. His popularity was international and continued well into the 20th century. His compositions included "parlor songs" ("Beautiful Dreamer") and songs for the black-face minstrel shows popular in the North which claimed to speak in the voice of Southern black people: "Swanee River," "Old Black Joe," and "Massa's in de Cold, Cold, Ground," for examples. "My Old Kentucky Home" reflects the thoughts of a black man who had been moved to the sugar fields of Louisiana. There used to be a statue in Louisville, Kentucky, dedicated to Foster, but it was a victim of the ethnic cleansing of 2020. Weep no more, My Lady.

My Old Kentucky Home

The sun shines bright in our old Kentucky home;

'Tis summer, the darkies are gay;

The corn-top's ripe, and the meadow's in the bloom,

While the birds make music all the day.

The young folks roll on the little cabin floor,

All merry, all happy, all bright;

By-'n'-by hard times comes a-knocking at the door:—

Then, my old Kentucky home, good night!

Weep no more, my lady,

O, weep no more to-day!

We will sing one song for my old Kentucky home,

For our old Kentucky home, far away.

They hunt no more for the possum and the coon,

On the meadow, the hill, and the shore;

They sing no more by the glimmer of the moon,

On the bench by the old cabin door:

The day goes by like a shadow o'er the heart,

With sorrow, where all was delight;
The time has come, when the darkies have to part:—
Then, my old Kentucky home, good night!
Weep no more, my lady,
O, weep no more to-day!
We will sing one song for the old Kentucky home,
For the old Kentucky home far away.

The head must bow, and the back will have to bend,
Wherever the darky may go;
A few more days, and the troubles all will end,
In the field where the sugar canes grow.
A few more days to tote the weary load,
No matter, 'twill will never be light;
A few more days till we totter on the road:—
Then, my old Kentucky home, good night!
Weep no more, my lady,
O, weep no more to-day!
We will sing one song for the old Kentucky home,
For the old Kentucky home far away.

♦ ♦ ♦

THEODORE O'HARA (1820 — 1867) of Kentucky. "The Bivouac of the Dead" is often thought of as related to The War of 1861-1865. Like the "Star-Spangled Banner" it was confiscated by the North. Theodore O'Hara was a Confederate officer. (He was with Gen. Albert Sidney Johnston when he was fatally wounded.) He wrote the poem about 1850 in commemoration of his comrades, the Kentucky volunteers who had lost their lives in the war with Mexico.

The Bivouac of the Dead

The muffled drum's sad roll has beat

The soldier's last tattoo;

No more on Life's parade shall meet

That brave and fallen few.

On fame's eternal camping ground

Their silent tents to spread,

And glory guards, with solemn round

The bivouac of the dead.

No rumor of the foe's advance

Now swells upon the wind;

Nor troubled thought at midnight haunts

Of loved ones left behind;

No vision of the morrow's strife

The warrior's dreams alarms;

No braying horn or screaming fife

At dawn shall call to arms.

Their shriveled swords are red with rust,

Their plumed heads are bowed,

Their haughty banner, trailed in dust,

Is now their martial shroud.
And plenteous funeral tears have washed
The red stains from each brow,
And the proud forms, by battle gashed
Are free from anguish now.

The neighing troop, the flashing blade,
The bugle's stirring blast,
The charge, the dreadful cannonade,
The din and shout, are past;
Nor war's wild note, nor glory's peal
Shall thrill with fierce delight
Those breasts that nevermore may feel
The rapture of the fight.
Like the fierce Northern hurricane
That sweeps the great plateau,
Flushed with triumph, yet to gain,
Come down the serried foe,
Who heard the thunder of the fray
Break o'er the field beneath,
Knew the watchword of the day
Was "Victory or death!"

Long had the doubtful conflict raged
O'er all that stricken plain,
For never fiercer fight had waged
The vengeful blood of Spain;
And still the storm of battle blew,

Still swelled the glory tide;
Not long, our stout old Chieftain knew,
Such odds his strength could bide.
Twas in that hour his stern command
Called to a martyr's grave
The flower of his beloved land,
The nation's flag to save.
By rivers of their father's gore
His first-born laurels grew,
And well he deemed the sons would pour
Their lives for glory too.

For many a mother's breath has swept
O'er Angostura's plain —
And long the pitying sky has wept
Above its moldered slain.
The raven's scream, or eagle's flight,
Or shepherd's pensive lay,
Alone awakes each sullen height
That frowned o'er that dread fray.

Sons of the Dark and Bloody Ground
Ye must not slumber there,
Where stranger steps and tongues resound
Along the heedless air.
Your own proud land's heroic soil
Shall be your fitter grave;
She claims from war his richest spoil —
The ashes of her brave.

Thus 'neath their parent turf they rest,
Far from the gory field,
Borne to a Spartan mother's breast
On many a bloody shield;
The sunshine of their native sky
Smiles sadly on them here,
And kindred eyes and hearts watch by
The heroes sepulcher.

Rest on embalmed and sainted dead!
Dear as the blood ye gave;
No impious footstep here shall tread
The herbage of your grave;
Nor shall your glory be forgot
While Fame her record keeps,
For honor points the hallowed spot
Where valor proudly sleeps.

Yon marble minstrel's voiceless stone
In deathless song shall tell,
When many a vanquished age has flown,
The story how ye fell;
Nor wreck, nor change, nor winter's blight,
Nor time's remorseless doom,
Can dim one ray of glory's light
That gilds your deathless tomb.

◆

The Old Pioneer

A dirge for the brave old pioneer!
Knight-errant of the wood!
Calmly beneath the green sod here
He rests from field and flood
The war-whoop and the panther's screams
No more his soul shall rouse,
For well the aged hunter dreams
Beside his good old spouse.

A dirge for the brave old pioneer!
Hushed now his rifle's peal;
The dews of many a vanish'd year
Are on his rusted steel;
His horn and pouch lie moldering
Upon the cabin-door;
The elk rests by the salted spring,
Nor flees the fierce wild boar.

A dirge for the brave old pioneer!
Old Druid of the West!
His offering was the fleet wild deer,
His shrine the mountain's crest.
Within his wildwood temple's space
An empire's towers nod,
Where erst, alone of all his race,
He knelt to Nature's God.

A dirge for the brave old pioneer!
Columbus of the land!
Who guided freedom's proud career
Beyond the conquer'd strand;
And gave her pilgrim sons a home
No monarch's step profanes,
Free as the chainless winds that roam
Upon its boundless plains.

A dirge for the brave old pioneer!
The muffled drum resound!
A Warrior is slumb'ring here
Beneath his battle-ground.
For not alone with beast of prey
The bloody strife he waged,
Foremost where'er the deadly fray
Of savage combat raged.

A dirge for the brave old pioneer!
A dirge for his old spouse!
For her who blest his forest cheer,
And kept his birchen house,
Now soundly by her chieftain may
The brave old dame sleep on,
The red man's step is far away,
The wolf's dread howl is gone.

A dirge for the brave old pioneer!
His pilgrimage is done;

He hunts no more the grizzly bear
About the setting sun.
Weary at last of chase and life,
He laid him here to rest,
Nor recks he now what sport or strife
Would tempt him further west.

A dirge for the brave old pioneer!
The patriarch of his tribe!
He sleeps—no pompous pile marks where,
No lines his deeds describe.
They raised no stone about him here,
Nor carved his deathless name —
An empire is his sepulchre,
His epitaph is Fame.

♦ ♦ ♦

ALEXANDER BEAUFORT MEEK (1814 — 1865) of Alabama. Meek was one of the most prominent citizens of antebellum Alabama—judge, orator, international chess master, and historian of the early days of his State. He also published two volumes of verse. Selections are from *The Songs and Poems of the South* (1857).

Come To The South

Oh, come to the South, sweet, beautiful one,

'Tis the clime of the heart, 'tis the shrine of the sun;

Where the sky ever shines with a passionate glow,

And flowers spread their treasures of crimson and snow;

Where the breeze, o'er bright waters, wafts incense along,

And gay birds are glancing in beauty and song;

Where summer smiles ever o'er mountain and plain,

And the best gifts of Eden, unshadowed, remain.

Oh, come to the South,

The shrine of the sun;

And dwell in its bowers,

Sweet, beautiful one.

Oh, come to the South, and I'll build thee a home,

Where winter shall never intrusively come,

The queen-like catalpa, the myrtle and pine,

The gold-fruited orange, the ruby-gemmed vine,

Shall bloom 'round thy dwelling, and shade thee at noon,

While birds of all music keep amorous tune;

By the gush of glad fountains we'll rest us at eve,

No trouble to vex us, no sorrows to grieve.

Oh, come to the South,

The shrine of the sun;

And dwell in its bowers,
Sweet, beautiful one.

Oh, come to the South, 'tis the home the heart—
No sky like its own can deep passion impart;
The glow of its summer felt in the soul,
And love keepeth ever his fervent control.
Oh, here would thy beauty most brilliantly beam,
And life pass away like some delicate dream;
Each wish of thy heart should realised be,
And this beautiful land seem an Eden to thee.
Then, come to the South,
The shrine of the sun;
And dwell in its bowers,
Sweet, beautiful one.

♦

The Mocking-Bird

From the vale, what music ringing,
Fills the bosom of the night,
On the sense, entranc'd, flinging
Spells of witchery and delight!
O'er magnolia, lime and cedar
From yon locust-top, it swells,
Like the chant of serenader,
Or the rhymes of silver bells!
Listen! dearest, listen to it!
Sweeter sounds were never heard!

'Tis the song of that wild poet—
Mime and minstrel—mocking-bird.
See him, swinging in his glory,
On yon topmost bending limb!
Carolling his amorous story,
Like some wild crusader's hymn!
Now it faints in tones delicious
As the first low vow of love!
Now it bursts in swells capricious,
All the moonlit vale above!

Why is't thus, this sylvan Petrarch
Pours all night his serenade?
'Tis for some proud woodland Laura,
His sad sonnets all are made!
But he changes now his measure—
Gladness bubbling from his mouth—
Jest, and gibe, and mimic pleasure—
Winged Anacreon of the South!
Listen! dearest, listen to it!
Sweeter sounds were never heard!
'Tis the song of that wild poet—
Mime and minstrel—mocking-bird.

Listen! dearest, listen to it!
Sweeter sounds were never heard!
'Tis the song of that wild poet—
Mime and minstrel—mocking-bird.

Bird of music, wit and gladness,
Troubadour of sunny climes,
Disenchanter of all sadness,—
Would thine art were in my rhymes,
O'er the heart that's beating by me,
I would weave a spell divine;
Is there aught she could deny me,
Drinking in such strains as thine?
Listen! dearest, listen to it!
Sweeter sounds were never heard
'Tis the song of that wild poet—
Mime and minstrel—mocking-bird.

◆

Choctaw Melodies 1

A Mother's Dirge For Her Infant

In a small grove of dogwood trees,
Whose spring-time flowers perfumed the breeze,
By Pascagoula's tawny wave,
There was a little new-made grave.
And there above the humble mound
A youthful mother oft was found,
Who thus, in sad and frantic strains,
Wept o'er her first-born babe's remains:
"Now cradled in the damp cold ground,

My little warrior lies;
Now he is bound with wampum round,
And shut his sparkling eyes:
Yet why, above his place of sleep—
Why should I weep?

"The little bird, when it is grown,
Must leave its native nest,
'Mid snares and foes to soar alone,
By want and care distrest;
And oft the cruel hunter's dart
Will pierce its heart.

"But thou, sweet one, hast shed no tears,
Nor felt the woes of life;
Thy spirit, undisturbed by fears,
By anguish and by strife,
To golden groves has soared above,
Bird of my love!

"Ah! hadst thou only staid below,
What grace and strength were thine,
To chase the dear, to bend the bow,
To draw the fisher's line!
Or bravely in the battle-field
The club to wield!
"Yet why should I lament thy doom?
The bud, that in the Spring-time dies,
Bears all its bloom and sweet perfume
To spirits in the skies!

A heavenly blossom now thou art,
Bud of my heart!

"But oh thou wert too young to go,—
Thy little tender feet
No father's guidance now can know,
No mother's counsel meet.
Who now will nurse thy fragile form,
And keep thee warm?

"Ah! yes, I hear a spirit say
I will protect him here—
Who from their cradles pass away,
To us are ever dear.
Then why my babe above thy sleep—
Why should I weep?"

♦

Choctaw Melodies 2

Atala's Lament
[From the French of Chateaubriand]

The Indian maiden turned at eve,
In exiled loneliness to grieve,
And shed, by Mississippi's side,
Her tears upon its turbid tide;
For she had left in passion's hours,
Her Florida's beloved bowers,
And thus, amid the stranger throng,
Poured forth an exile's plaintive song:

"Oh, happy they who ne'er have seen
The smoke of alien fires!
Nor guests at other feasts have been,
Than their own sires'!
Ah! should the blue-jay of the West
Say to the Southern nonpareil,
'Why not amid our branches rest?
Why only mourning numbers tell?
Have we not limpid waters here—
Delightful shades, abundant food,
And flowery fields, and orchards fair,
As you have in your native wood?'
Yet would the stray bird answer then,
'My nest is in the jasmine grove!
Oh, give my golden skies agen,
And bright savannahs that I love!'

"Oh, happy they who ne'er have seen
The smoke of alien fires,
Nor guests at other feasts have been,
Than their own sires'!
When, after hours of toil and pain,
The weary traveler sinks at night,
And sees anear him, on the plain,
Fair cottages with many a light;
In vain he views their pleasant glow—
No hospitable fare they yield—
For, should he enter with his bow,

All welcome is at once concealed;
Again his sturdy bow he takes,
And, weak, insulted, turns away,
And totters on through tangled brakes,
And deserts wide till dawn of day.

"Oh, happy they who ne'er have seen
The smoke of alien fires,
Nor guests at other feasts have been,
Than their own sires'!
Dear stories round the social hearth!
Soft songs with tenderest feelings rife!
Pure deeds of love, and tones of mirth,
So needful in this weary life!—
Ye, ye have filled the days of those
Who ne'er their parent land have left,—
Who ne'er have been, 'mid stranger foes,
Of all that's best on earth bereft!
They live in bliss, and when life ends,
Their graves are in their mother's breast;
By setting suns and tears of friends,
And fair religion sweetly blest!
Oh, happy they who ne'er have seen
The smoke of alien fires,
Nor guests at other feasts have been,
Than their own sires'!"

◆

The Rose of Alabama

I loved, in boyhood's happy time,
When life was like a minstrel's rhyme,
And cloudless as my native clime,
The Rose of Alabama.
Oh, lovely rose!
The sweetest flower earth knows,
Is the Rose of Alabama!

One pleasant, balmy night in June,
When swung, in silvery clouds, the moon,
My heart awoke love's vesper tune,
For Rose of Alabama!
She caught the strain, and to the bower,
Impelled by love and music's power,
Stole like an angel, at that hour,
The Rose of Alabama!

Beside me there her form she placed,
My arm stole gently 'round her waist,
And earth seemed with new beauty graced,
By Rose of Alabama!
The breeze and streamlet ceased their tone;
Like winged gems the fire-flies shone;
The flowers gazed envious on my own
Sweet Rose of Alabama!

'Tis vain our mutual vows to tell—
One strain upon my plaintive shell,

And then I bade a sad farewell
To Rose of Alabama!
Long years have passed; by fortune driven,
I wander 'neath a stranger heaven;
But, ah! love's ties are not yet riven
From Rose of Alabama!

Hope smiles upon my pilgrim way,
Ere long my feet shall homeward stray,
And time bring round my nuptial day
With Rose of Alabama!
Then, shrine-like, in my native land,
Love's Eden! shall my cottage stand,
With happiness on every hand!
Sweet Rose of Alabama!

◆

The Homes of Alabama

The homes of Alabama,
How beautiful they rise,
Throughout her queenly forest realm,
Beneath her smiling skies!
The richest odors fill the breeze,
Her vallies teem with wealth,
And the homes of Alabama,
Are the rosy homes of health!

The homes of Alabama,—
The cottage and the hall,—

Her institutions spread alike
A guardian care o'er all!—
No titled fopling spurns aside
The peasant from his way,
But the homes of Alabama
Are blessed by equal sway!

The homes of Alabama,
The prairie's flowery bed,—
The broad fields decked with snowy wreaths,—
The mountain's star-crowned head:
The forest and the fertile soil,
Each, all, their tributes bring,
And the homes of Alabama,
Teem with the offering!

The homes of Alabama,
The shrines of Faith and Love,
Where honest hearts forever lift
Their incense-prayers above!
Where science, art and peace combine
To scatter bliss around,
And make the once rude savage wastes
Now consecrated ground!

The homes of Alabama,
Homes of the Brave and Free,—
Stout hearts beneath their cabin roofs
Pulsate with liberty!

They scorn the despot's iron rule,
The zealot's galling chain,—
And the homes of Alabama
Shall ever free remain!
The homes of Alabama,
Let the tyrant keep his own,
The bigot nurse his narrow creed,
But not pollute her zone!
Should War and Frenzy ever strive
To crush her strength, they'll feel
That the homes of Alabama
Are filled by hearts of steel!

♦

Land of The South

LAND of the South! — imperial land! —
How proud thy mountains rise!
How sweet thy scenes on every hand!
How fair thy covering skies!
But not for this — oh, not for these —
I love thy fields to roam;
Thou hast a dearer spell to me, —
Thou art my native home!
Thy rivers roll their liquid wealth,
Unequaled to the sea;
Thy hills and valleys bloom with health,
And green with verdure be!
But not for thy proud ocean streams,
Not for thy azure dome,

Sweet, sunny South, I cling to thee, —
Thou art my native home!
I've stood beneath ltalia's clime,
Beloved of tale and song,
On Helvyn's hills, proud and sublime,
Where nature's wonders throng;
By Tempe's classic sunlit streams,
Where Gods, of old, did roam, —
But ne'er have found so fair a land
As thou, my native home!
And thou hast prouder glories, too,
Than nature ever gave;
Peace sheds o'er thee her genial dew,
And Freedom's pinions wave;
Fair Science flings her pearls around,
Religion lifts her dome, —
These, these endear thee to my heart,
My own, loved native home!
And "Heaven's best gift to man" is thine —
God bless thy rosy girls!
Like sylvan flowers they sweetly shine,
Their hearts are pure as pearls!
And grace and goodness circle them,
Where'er their footsteps roam;
How can I then, whilst loving them,
Not love my native home?
Land of the South! — imperial land! —
Then here's a health to thee:
Long as thy mountain barriers stand,

May'st thou be blest and free!
May dark dissension's banner ne'er
Wave o'er thy fertile loam!
But should it come, there's one will die
To save his native home!

♦

Ireland
(1848)

While thus our country, in her eagle flight,
Bears proudly upward to the Orb of Light,
Shall we, her sons, forget the claims of those,
Who now are struggling with oppression's woes?
No, o'er the waters of the Atlantic deep,
Our warmest sympathies, like ark-doves, sweep,
And, to the sufferers of the Emerald Isle,
Would bear the branch of love, and freedom's smile!
The land of Grattan, Curran, Emmet, Tone,—
The trampled footstool of a foreign throne!
Oh, blood of martyrs!—staining all her green,
Soon may ye wash her spotted garments clean!
The harp of Tara!—soon may it pour forth
The olden anthems through the island-north!—
And Emmet's epitaph ring o'er the sea—
"Erin Mavourneen!—thou art free—art free!"

♦ ♦ ♦

THOMAS HOLLEY CHIVERS (1809 — 1858) of Georgia was a physician and poet and a friend of Edgar Allan Poe, who encouraged him. He published over 10 volumes of poetry and plays but was largely forgotten until rediscovered by 20th century critics. Chivers believed that good poetry was a result of"divine inspiration."

Faith

Faith is the flower that blooms unseen

By mountains of immortal green—

A hoped-for harvest in the skies,

In which the reaper never dies—

A tree to which the power is given

To lift its branches into heaven;

And from whose boughs of gorgeous fruit

A loftier tree shall take its root.

Lord! we are grafted into thine,

When broken off from Adam's vine;

And so, from that degenerate tree,

We grow into the life of thee!

For, by the prunings of thy word,

Are we then purged into the Lord;

And like Mount Zion we shall stand

The Temples of our native land.

Lord! if the stars should take their flight,

And vanish from the halls of night;

And if the morning should appear,

And vanish from the evening near;

And if the rivers should run dry,

And every flower that decks them die;

And if the world should cease to be—

I would not lose my trust in Thee.

♦

The Voice of Thought

Faint as the far-down tone
Beneath the sounding sea,
Muffled, by its own moan,
To silent melody;
So faint we cannot tell
But that the sound we hear
Is some sweet roses' smell
That falls upon our ear;
(As if the Butterfly
Shaking the Lily-bell,
While drinking joyfully,
Should toll its own death-knell!)
Sweeter than Hope's sweet lute
Singing of joys to be,
When Pain's harsh voice is mute,
Is the Soul's sweet song to me.

♦

To Idealon
(To Edgar Allan Poe)

Soul of the sunny South! thy voice is heard
In the deep stillness of the virgin heart!
Thy name is coupled with that heavenly word,
And never from her chambers shall depart!
A soothing voice—whose tones shall never die!
Soul of the sunny South! let not thy lays,
Flung on the waters, perish in the sea!

No! let them come back after many days,
To feed the heart that once was life to thee!
Go—like the turtle that has left her grove,
And pour thy spirit upon those that love.

♦

Song Of The Maids Of Texas
(1837)

Awake, love, awake! for the morning is high,
And the sunbeams are bright in the vault of the sky—
The trumpet is heard by the isles of the sea,
Then awake, love, awake! for my soul is with thee!
The roses are wet with the dews of the night,
And the day-dawn is crowning the hills with delight;
The roebucks are making their tracks in the sand,
"And the voice of the turtle is heard in our land."
Awake, love, awake! for the dews of the morn
Are dashed from the boughs by the sound of the horn—
The autumn is gone, and the winter is past,
And the ring-doves are heard in the valleys at last;
The rose-buds are bright in the light of the dew,
And the sage-bells are blooming with nectar for you;
The cymbal-bee drinks from the chalice at hand,
"And the voice of the turtle is heard in our land."
Awake, love, awake! for the young fawns are nigh,
And the last star is gone from its home in the sky—
The lily-bells shine in the valleys below,
And the sweet William shakes by the foot of the roe;

The snow-pigeon hies from the hill-tops to feed,
And the blackbirds are singing their songs in the mead—
Awake, love, awake, for my heart and my hand,
"For the voice of the turtle is heard in our land."

♦

Hymn To The Deity

"Heal me, oh! Lord! and I shall be healed; and save me,
and I shall be saved; for Thou art my praise." —Jer. 17:14.

Lord! let the rivers of Thy love,

Pour down upon me from above;

Let the bright waves of glory roll

Around this Sanctuary of my soul.

Let not the Island-clouds that lie

In the Pavilion of the sky

Gather around my Dwelling-place,

And hide the glory of Thy face.

Thou art upon the raging seas,

And in the whispers of the breeze;

And in the lightnings of the sky,

Filling the firmament on high.

Thou art upon the mighty hills,

And in the music of the rills;

And in the whirlwinds of the sea,

And in the voice that speaks to Thee.

Thou art upon the darkest night,

And in the brightest of the light;

And in the Highest Heaven, as well

And in the lowest depths of Hell.
Thus, seeing that Thy Home is here,
And feeling that Thy voice is near;
And knowing what Thy strength must be—
I offer up my prayer to Thee!

♦ ♦ ♦

MARY E. WILSON BETTS of Kentucky was a prolific and valued poet in journals of her time. Not a lot is known about her except that she was married in 1854 and died young. The poem concerns Col. William L. Crittenden of Kentucky who took part in the failed Lopez insurrection in Cuba in 1851. He was captured and executed by the Spanish.

A Kentuckian Kneels To None But God

Ah! tyrants forge your chains at will—

Nay! gall this flesh of mine:

Yet, thought is free, unfettered still,

And will not yield to thine!

Take, take the life that Heaven gave,

And let my heart's blood stain thy sod.

But know ye not Kentucky's brave

Will kneel to none but God?

You've quenched fair freedom's sunny light,

Her music tones have stilled,

And with a deep and darkened blight,

The trusting heart have filled!

Then do you think that I will kneel

Where such as you have trod?

Nay! point your cold and threatening steel—

I'll kneel to none but God.

As summer breezes lightly rest

Upon a quiet river,

And gently on its sleeping breast

The moonbeams softly quiver—

Sweet thoughts of home light up my brow

When goaded with the rod;

Yet, these cannot unman me now—

I'll kneel to none but God.
And tho' a sad and mournful tone
Is coldly sweeping by;
And dreams of bliss forever flown
Have dimmed with tears mine eye—
Yet, mine's a heart unyielding still—
Heap on my breast the clod;
My soaring spirit scorns thy will—
I'll kneel to none but God.

♦ ♦ ♦

LOUISA SUSANNAH CHEVES McCORD (1810 — 1879) of South Carolina was one of the most outstanding women of 19th century America. She was the daughter of Langdon Cheves, who had been Speaker of the U.S. House of Representatives and had held other important posts. In the antebellum period, while a plantation mistress, she published poetry, strong polemical essays in Southern reviews, a 5-act play (1851), and she made the first English language translation of the work of the French free market economist Frederic Bastiat (1848). During the war she was a mainstay of Confederate hospitals and poor relief in Columbia. Her Columbia house, which still stands, was ransacked but it was not burned in the destruction of Columbia because it was used as a headquarters by the odious Yankee general O.O. Howard. Presented here is a passage from her play *Caius Gracchus*. The complaints of the Roman tribune against the wealthy reflects a protest to the North's arrogant exploitation of the South.

From The Address Of Gracchus
In Act I, Scene VI

Friends, brothers, Roman citizens, I come

As ye have willed it, that I may explain

And speak to you concerning your own rights.

Man has, in every station, rights his due.

Our slaves look to their masters for support.

The very claims we hold upon their labour

Make us a rule to tender them again

What comforts we can furnish to their lot.

If placed by circumstance, necessity,

Beneath our rule, protection thence we owe—

And he basely evading these, degrades

Himself below the thus defrauded slave.

You, Romans, have a sterner government;

For our rich nobles, who do make themselves

Perforce the country's purse-holders, forget

To leave some portion of your gains for you
Whose toil and heart-ache won them. Are ye poor?
Why do your starving infants beg in vain
A hard, dry crust? Why are their shivering limbs
Wrapt but in rags, as they cower tearful round
The dying embers of your empty hearths?
Are there no vacant lands, the people's due?
Where are the rich fields that your fathers conquered?
And where the exuberant harvests that yourselves
Have made Rome's property? What justice gave them
New riches to the rich? The proud patrician
Who toiled not, bled not, in the gaining them;
Who sat at home by the fire and warmed himself
By talking over battles that you fought;
He waited for no law to make them his;
But by the strong hand of oppression seizes
The bread which should have fed your hungry babes.
Is there no corn in the market? You will find
A large abundance. There have lately been
New importations from the provinces.
Why do you starve, then? Why do you not buy?
You smile as though the bare idea were strange.
You cannot buy. You have no monies. Rich,
Usurious, the plunderer speculates
On your starvation. Beggars the which you are
His robberies make you, and he taunts you then,
Mocking your poverty by this display,
Showing how rich the country is in grain,
While he from hunger-clenched fingers, screws

To pay for a mere handful, your last doit!
With poverty your chilling bed-fellow,
And hugged by hunger, while ye thus are driven
To wrap ye in your rags and wait for death,
Who are those laborers, well-dressed, happy, sleek,
Tilling the fields which, citizens, are yours?
From the depopulated country fly
The shepherd and the husbandman, to make
Room for the rich man's slave. Beasts have their dens,
They hide them in their caves, and there may rest;
But you, who in the cause of Italy
Your heart's-blood spill, ye Roman citizens—
To you she gives no home! She leaves you nought
Save only God's light and the air you breathe!
The poor man has no home; he claims no shed
'Neath which his huddling brats may gather them.
From place to place the forlorn things he drags
And with their mother lays them on the earth
There, where the soldier sleeps. What mockery then,
To call on such, ye generals of Rome,
And bid them fight for their domestic Gods,
Their homes and sepulchres! Their sepulchres!
Their fathers' bones are scattered to the winds
And the patrician ploughs them through his fields,
Nor heeds plebeian graves! And yet they fight;
Plebeians fight and die. The Roman blood
Boils up in the combat and the victory's won,
For what? That these proud rich may sit and revel
In some new luxury, some dear-bought pleasure,

While you, ye so-called masters of the world,
In your possession hold no foot of ground!
To your assistance you have summoned me;
And where the anxious thought you dared not word,
Your walls speak to me. Public monuments
In blotted and scrawled sentences implore
Succor to Rome. Dare ye then help yourselves?
On you I call, to make your effort too.

♦ ♦ ♦

ALBERT PIKE (1809 — 1891) of Arkansas, though born in Boston, adventured to the frontier as a young man. He served in the Mexican War, was chief legal counsel to the Five Civilised Tribes and a Confederate general. He was already well-known as a poet before the War, during which his verses really flourished, as will be seen in the Confederate poets volumes of this series.

Ode

(July 4, 1853)

When shall the nations all be free,

And Force no longer reign;

None bend to brutal Power the knee,

None hug the gilded chain?

No longer rule the ancient Wrong,

The Weak be trampled by the Strong?—

How long, dear God in heaven! how long,

The people wail in vain?

Do not th' Archangels on their thrones,

Turn piteous looks to Thee,

When round them thickly swarm the groans

Of those that would be free?

Of those that know they have the right

To Freedom, though crushed down by Might,

As all the world hath to the light

And air which Thou mad'st free?

The ancient Empires staggering drift

Along Time's mighty tide,

Whose waters, running broad and swift,

Eternity divide:

How many years shall pass, before
Over their bones the sea shall roar,
The salt sand drift, the fresh rains pour,
The stars mock fallen Pride?

What then the Great Republic's fate?
To founder far from land,
And sink with all her glorious freight,
Smitten by God's right hand?
Or shall she still her helm obey
In calm or storm, by night or day,
No sail rent, no spar cut away
Exultant, proud and grand?
The issues are with God. To do,
Of right belongs to us:
May we be ever just and true,
For nations flourish thus!—
JUSTICE is mightier than ships;
RIGHT, than the cannon's brazen lips;
And TRUTH, averting dark eclipse,
Makes fortunes prosperous.

♦

To The Mocking Bird

Thou glorious mocker of the world! I hear
Thy many voices ringing through the glooms
Of these green solitudes; and all the clear,
Bright joyance of their song enthralls the ear,
And floods the heart. Over the sphered tombs
Of vanished nations rolls thy music-tide;
No light from History's starlit page illumes
The memory of these nations; they have died:
None care for them but thou; and thou mayst sing
O'er me, perhaps, as now thy clear notes ring
Over their bones by whom thou once was deified.

Glad scorners of all cities; Thou dost leave
The world's mad turmoil and incessant din,
Where none in other's honesty believe,
Where the old sigh, the young turn gray and grieve,
Where misery gnaws the maiden's heart within:
Thou fleest far into the dark green woods,
Where, with thy flood of music, thou can'st win
Their heart to harmony, and where intrudes
No discord on thy melodies. Oh, where,
Among the sweet musicians of the air
Is one so dear as thou to these old solitudes?
Ha! what a burst was that! The Aeolian strain
Goes floating through the tangled passages
Of the still woods, and now it comes again,

A multitudinous melody,—like a rain
Of glassy music under echoing trees,
Close by a ringing lake. It wraps the soul
With a bright harmony of happiness,
Even as a gem is wrapped when round it roll
Thin waves of crimson flame; till we become
With the excess of perfect pleasure, dumb,
And pant like a swift runner clinging to the goal.

I cannot love the man who doth not love,
As men love light, the song of happy birds;
For the first visions that my boy-heart wove
To fill its sleep with, were that I did rove
Through the fresh woods, what time the snowy herds
Of morning clouds shrunk from the advancing sun
Into the depths of Heaven's blue heart, as words
From the Poet's lips float gently, one by one,
And vanish in the human heart; and then
I revelled in such songs, and sorrowed when,
With noon-heat overwrought, the music gush was done.

I would, sweet bird, that I might live with thee,
Amid the eloquent grandeur of these shades,
Alone with nature, but it may not be;
I have to struggle with the stormy sea
Of human life until existence fades
Into death's darkness. Thou wilt sing and soar
Through the thick woods and shadow checkered glades,

While pain and sorrow cast no dimness o'er
The brilliance of thy heart; but I must wear,
As now, my garments of regret and care,—
As penitents of old their galling sack cloth wore.

Yet why complain? What though fond hopes deferred
Have overshadowed Life's green paths with gloom?
Content's soft music is not all unheard;
There is a voice sweeter than thine, sweet bird,
To welcome me within my humble home;
There is an eye, with love's devotion bright,
The darkness of existence to illume.
Then why complain? When death shall cast his blight
Over the spirit, my cold bones shall rest
Beneath these trees; and, from thy swelling breast,
Over them pour thy song, like a rich flood of light.

◆

The Dead Child

The young leaf lives in Spring its little hour,
And falleth from the limb— who knoweth why?
The fair young bud blooms not into a flower,
But sickening droops and hasteneth to die.
Who knoweth why?
Our Father knows, from whom the bud and leaf
Received their life, so beautiful and brief.

Those loved by us, the young, fair, innocent,—
When like your dear ones they have grown more dear
For but a little season to us lent,
He calleth home, letting us live on here—
Who knoweth why?
They in the early morning of Life's day
Do fade and fade, while we grow old and gray.

Our Father knows. He knew they did not need
Life's discipline and sorrow's chastening pain
To make them fit for Heaven, and early freed
These pure white souls to Him returned again
For us to intercede.
Thus we, amid Life's sorrows, toils and cares,
Have entertained His angels unawares.

♦

The Fall Of Poland 1832

She has sunken again into slavery's tomb,
Like a thunderbolt quenching itself in the sea;
And deeply and darkly engraved is her doom,—
"Her existence is done! Let her never be free!'

From the darkness that long eddied round her she rose,
And flinging her grave-clothes of bondage aside,
A brave, bold defiance she hurled at her foes;
And her shot-riddled flag flew once more in its pride.

'Twas the battle of RIGHT against Outrage and Wrong,
The last noble struggle for life and free laws;
And every heart to whose feelings belong
Any generous impulses, prayed for her cause.

As the clouds of a tropical hurricane roll
From horizon to zenith, so swelled her array;
As the broad fields of ice drifting south from the pole,
So gathered her forces, all fierce for the fray.

For each manly heart in which beat the free blood
Of a true Polack joyfully rushed to the ranks;
Then forth to the frontier they rolled, like a flood
That, swelled with great rains, overflows all its banks.

And lo! the old flag proudly waved in the air,
Over city and plain, as of yore was its wont;
And the souls of her mighty departed were there,
Like the shades of dead gods, marching on in the front.

But the fetters are clasped on her limbs once again,
And riveted strongly, and clenched there forever;
Sad, sad, is her soul, sharp and bitter her pain,
And dark the deep dungeons where light wandereth never.

Oh, shame on you! shame on you, children of Gaul!
You had just become free, and you might have been great;

But you suffered the noblest of nations to fall,
And lie bleeding and maimed at the merciless gate

Of the grim Northern Wolf, whose white teeth, dripping red,
Yet mangle the corpse of the stag he has slain.
Shame! shame! a proud people were better be dead,
Than disgraced by ingratitude's ignoble stain.

When a word from your mouth, like the lightning's swift flame,
Would have sent back the Wolf to his lair in the snow,
And made the dull hater of Freedom as tame
As his serfs, that smile thanks in return for a blow.

When you might have been hailed the true kings of the world,
And your memory ever regarded with love;
Had you struck but one blow, but one cannon-shot hurled,
The thunders of God would have helped from above.

That then you should heed not their earnest appeal,
Who under Napoleon fought by your side,
Nor think that you saw, through the glitter of steel,
Brave Poniatowski rejoicingly ride!

Live on, then, and crouch to your Citizen King!
This tale of your baseness shall often be sung;
And its memory, a halo of shame, round you cling,
To be never thrown off while the world has a tongue.

♦

France 1829

Wake! children of France! shall your tyrant forever
Enslave and enchain you, and trample you down?
Do you fear the sharp fetters that gall you to sever,
And tear from the brow of the despot his crown?

Up! children of France! Let the flag that you honor,
Be once more the flag of the free and the brave!
Your country is chained; the Philistines are on her;
Who heeds not her call is both coward and knave.

If you have but one spark of the spirit that lighted
The souls of your fathers, exhibit it now;
And sheathe not the sword till your wrongs are all righted,
Though blood to the reins of your horses should flow.

Ye fear not the throne, nor its base truckling minions;
On, on to the contest with cuirass and lance!
Till your eagles again spread their conquering pinions,
And peace and security reign over France.

Let the pale monarchs quake! for their thrones shall be
shaken!
Let them league once again, as they leagued once before!
Their fury and madness, when France shall awaken,
Will be like the ocean-wave chafing the shore.

Up! men of gay France!—Your poor children upbraid you,
Your gray-headed parents cry out on your shame:
Up! up! and your ancestors' spirits will aid you,
Your tyrant to humble, your taskmaker tame.

Strike, children of France! strike for freedom and glory,
As ye and your fathers have stricken before;
Ye may fall, but your names shall be blazoned in story,
To beacon the free through the hurricane's roar.

Black Eagle of Russia! thy pride shall be lowered,
When France and her armies are roused for the fray;
And Austria shall cower again, as she cowered
When the Corsican swept her great armies away.

Up! arm for the contest! Your foes are around you;
The foot of your king presses hard on your hearts;
The Pigmies came, while you were sleeping, and bound you:
Strike once, ere occasion forever departs!

One blow! but one blow!—for your long years of anguish!
Your children, your parents, your own honest fame!
Or will you through ages of agony languish,—
To be cowards at heart. Frenchmen only in name?

♦ ♦ ♦

HENRY ROOTES JACKSON (1820 — 1898) of Georgia was a lawyer, soldier, diplomat, judge, and poet. He was U.S. Minister to Austrai/ Hungary 1853-1858 and was well-known for prosecuting Yankee slave traders trying to import African captives into Savannah shortly before the war. He was Colonel of the 1st Georgia Volunteers in the Mexican War and fought the Confederate army throughout the war, becoming a brigadier general. After the war he was appointed by President Cleveland as the U.S. Minister to Mexico. In 1880 he published a book of poems *Talulah*. The third selection reflects a soldier's thoughts.

The Red Old Hills Of Georgia

The red old hills of Georgia!

So bald, and bare, and bleak—

Their memory fills my spirit

With thoughts I cannot speak.

They have no robe of verdure,

Stript naked to the blast;

And yet, of all the varied earth,

I love them best at last.

I love them for the pleasure

With which my lift was blest,

When erst I left in boyhood

My footsteps on their breast.

When in the rains had perished

Those steps from plain and knoll,

Then vanished, with the storm of grief,

Joy's footprints from my soul!

The red old hills of Georgia!
My heart is on them now;
Where, fed from golden streamlets,
Oconee's waters flow!
I love them with devotion,
Though washed so bleak and bare—
Oh! can my spirit e'er forget
The warm hearts dwelling there?

I love them for the living—
The generous, kind, and gay;
And for the dead who slumber
Within their breasts of clay.
I love them for the bounty
Which cheers the social hearth;
I love them for their rosy girls—
The fairest on the earth!

The red old hills of Georgia!
Oh! where upon the face
Of earth is freedom's spirit
More bright in any race?
In Switzerland and Scotland
Each patriot breast it fills,
But oh! it blazes brighter yet
Among our Georgia hills!

And where, upon their surface,
Is heart to feeling dead?
Oh! when has needy stranger
Gone from those hills unfed?
There bravery and kindness
For aye, go hand in hand,

Upon your washed and naked hills,
My own, my native land!

The red old hills of Georgia
I never can forget;
Amid life's joys and sorrows,
My heart is on them yet;
And when my course has ended—
No more to toil or rove,
May I be held in their dear clasp
Close, close to them I love!

♦

The Mountains In Georgia

Ye glorious Alleghanies! from this height
I see your peaks on every side arise;
Their summits roll beneath the giddy sight,
Like ocean billows heaved among the skies.
in wild magnificence upon them lies
The primal forest—kindling in the glow

Of this mild autumn sun with golden dyes,
While, in his slanting ray, their shadows grow
Broad o'er the paradise of vale and wood below.

How beautiful! though, fresh from Nature's God,
They show no footstep of an elder race;
No human hand has ever turned their sod,
Or heaved their massive granite from its place;
The green banks of their floods bear not a trace
Of pomp and power, which have come and gone,
And left their crumbling ruins to deface
The virgin earth. Here Nature rules alone;
The beauty of the hill and valley is her own.

Nor might the future generations know
Aught of the simple people who have made
Their habitations by the streams that flow
So fresh and stainless from the forest shade,
Who built their council fires on hill and glade,
And in yon pleasant valleys, by the fall
Of crystal founts, perchance, their dead have laid;
But for the names of mountain, river, cataract—all
Significant of thought and sweetly musical.

♦

My Wife And Child

The tattoo beats; the lights are gone;
The camp around in slumber lies;
The night with solemn pace moves on;
The shadows thicken o'er the skies;
But sleep my weary eyes hath flown,
And sad, uneasy thoughts arise.

I think of thee, oh! dearest one!
Whose love my early life hath blest;
Of thee and him—our baby son—
Who slumbers on thy gentle breast;
God of the tender, frail and lone,
Oh! guard that little sleeper's rest!
Wherever fate those forms may throw,
Loved with a passion almost wild—
By day, by night—in joy or woe—
By fears oppressed, or hopes beguiled—
From every danger, every foe,
O God! protect my wife and child!

♦ ♦ ♦

FRANCIS ORRAY TICKNOR (1822 — 1876) of Georgia was a highly regarded physician trained in Philadelphia and a contributor of scientific articles to agricultural publications. He was already established as a poet before the War as these antebellum verses show. He also wrote some of the most memorable Confederate poetry which will appear in *The Land They Loved. Confederate Poets and Poetry.* His "Little Giffen" is among the greatest verse to come out of the Confederacy.

E. P. C. - A Lily Of The Valley

Thy smile, sweet sister, on my lay,

Is as the stars, I ween,

That brightens o'er this brilliant's ray,

Which, else, no light had seen!

That kindles o'er some brooklet's way,

Where, else, no song had been!

If aught of summer worth it brings

In bloom or melodies,

'Tis little for the lyric wings

Thy radiance taught to rise,

But little for a bird that sings

So near his Paradise.

By Hope in many a broken home,

And by the tears that shed

The proudest splendor of the tomb

Above the humblest head,

This song but asks thy soul's perfume

To crown our Quick and Dead.

♦

Home

FOREST-GIRDED, cedar-scented,
Veiled like Vesper, sweet and dim;
Pure as burned the Temple's glory,
Shadowed by the Seraphim;
Islet from contending oceans,
Coral-cinctured, crowned with palm,
Where the wrestling world's commotions
Melt through music into calm;
Throats that sing and wings that flutter
Softly 'mid the balm and bloom;
Sweeter sounds than lip can utter
Hath my heart for thee,
My home.

Bless that dear old Angel Saxon
For the sounds he formed so well;
Little words, the nectar-waxen
Harvest of a honey-cell,
Sealing all a summer's sweetness
In a single syllable!
For, of all his quaint word-building,
The queen-cell of all the comb
Is that grand old Saxon mouthful,
Dear old Saxon heartful,
Home.

◆

To A Lady Of Texas, In Italy
(Mrs. William Maverick.)

A thousand leagues of steam and foam,
To breathe, tho' but an hour, in Rome!
To wake in Florence, or to be
Cradled in Venice by the sea!
Yet sometimes, lady, when thine eyes
Are weary of yon wondrous skies,
With all thy pulses languid grown
To miracles in stain and stone,
Seek thou some sacred fountain dim,
A mirror with its marble rim,
And bend thy "sunbeam" face to see
The fairest thing in Italy!
Yea, lovelier than the sunset seas
Kindled, to guide the Genoese!

♦

Unknown

The prints of feet are worn away,
No more the mourners come;
The voice of wail is mute to-day
As his whose life is dumb.

The world is bright with other bloom;
Shall the sweet summer shed
Its living radiance o'er the tomb
That shrouds the doubly dead?

Unknown! Beneath our Father's face
The star-lit hillocks lie:
Another rosebud! lest His grace
Forget us when we die.

◆ ◆ ◆

WILLIAM HENRY TIMROD (1792 — 1838) of South Carolina was a captain of volunteers who went from Charleston to the defense of St. Augustine in the Second Seminole War. He was a bookbinder and bookseller whose offices were a gathering place for Charleston's literary circle. William Gilmore Simms described him as "a strong man, of quick intellect, at once sparkling and sensitive." "Harry" is, of course, about his son Henry. Tradition says that the father, at the boy's birth, predicted he would be a poet.

To Time, The Old Traveler

They slander thee, Old Traveler,
>Who say that thy delight
Is to scatter ruin, far and wide,
>In thy wantonness of might
For not a leaf that falleth
>Before thy restless wings,
But in thy flight, thou changest it
>To a thousand brighter things.

Thou passest o'er the battlefield
>Where the dead lie stiff and stark,
Where naught is heard save the vulture's scream,
>And the gaunt wolf's famished bark;
But thou hast caused the grain to spring
>From the blood-enriched clay,
And the waving corn-tops seem to dance
>To the rustic's merry lay.

Thou hast strewed the lordly palace
>In ruins on the ground,
And the dismal screech of the owl is heard
>Where the harp was wont to sound;

But the selfsame 'spot thou coverest
    With the dwellings of the poor,
And a thousand happy hearts enjoy
    What one usurped before.

'T is true thy progress layeth
    Full many a loved one low,
And for the brave and beautiful
    Thou hast caused our tears to flow;
But always near the couch of death
    Nor thou, nor we can stay;
And the breath of thy departing wings,
    Dries all our tears away !

◆

The Mocking-Bird

            Nor did lack
Sweet music to the magic of the scene:
The little crimson-breasted Nonpareil
Was there, his tiny feet scarce bending down
The silken tendril, that he lighted on
To pour his love notes; and in russet coat,
Most homely, like true genius bursting forth
In spite of adverse fortune, a full choir
Within himself, the merry Mock Bud sate,
Filling the air with melody; and at times,
In the rapt favour of his sweetest song
Be quivering form would spring into the sky,
In spiral circles, as if he would catch

New powers from kindred warblers in the clouds
Who would bend down to greet him!

♦

To Harry

HARRY, my little blue-eyed boy,
    I love to have thee playing near;
There's music in thy shouts of joy
    To a fond father's ear.

I love to see the lines of mirth
    Mantle thy cheek and forehead fair,
As if all pleasures of the earth
    Had met to revel there;

For gazing on thee, do I sigh
    That those most happy years must flee,
And thy full share of misery
    Must fall in life on thee!
There is no lasting grief below,
    My Harry! that flows not from guilt;
Thou canst not read my meaning now—
    In after times thou wilt.

Thou 'lt read it when the churchyard clay
    Shall lie upon thy father's breast,
And he, though dead, will point the way
    Thou shalt be always blest.

♦ ♦ ♦

HENRY TIMROD (1828 — 1867) of South Carolina was well-established as one of America's foremost lyric poets before the war, but the great subject of Southern independence brought forth his best works. Timrod, though suffering from incipient tuberculosis, twice enlisted in the Confederate army but both times was discharged as unfit. Poverty and hardship endured while struggling to support his family in the ruins of Columbia hastened Timrod's death at thirty-nine. A few months before, he had written "The Ode to the Confederate Dead," for the occasion of placing flowers on the Confederate graves at Magnolia Cemetery in Charleston, until then forbidden by the U.S. Army. Some people claim to prefer the vicious and blasphemous "Battle Hymn of the Republic" or Walt Whitman's adolescent jingles, but for my money Timrod's "Ode to the Confederate Dead" is the most magnificent piece of literature to come out of The War. His work will be featured in later volumes of Confederate Poets.

Sonnets

I

Poet! if on a lasting fame be bent

Thy unperturbing hopes, thou will not roam

Too far from thine own happy heart and home;

Cling to the lowly earth, and be content!

So shall thy name be dear to many a heart;

So shall the noblest truths by thee be taught;

The flower and fruit of wholesome human thought,

Bless the sweet labors of thy gentle art.

The brightest stars are nearest to the earth,

And we may track the mighty sun above,

Even by the shadow of a slender. flower.

Always, O bard, humility is power!

And thou mayst draw from matters of the hearth

Truths wide as nations, and as deep as love.

II

Most men know love but as a part of life;
They hide it in some corner of the breast,
Even from themselves; and only when they rest
In the brief pauses of that daily strife,
Wherewith the world might else be not so rife,
They draw it forth (as one draws forth a toy
To soothe some ardent, kiss-exacting boy)
And hold it up to sister, child, or wife.
Ah me! why may not love and life be one?
Why walk we thus alone, when by our side,
Love, like a visible God, might be our guide?
How would the marts grow noble! and the street,
Worn like a dungeon-floor by weary feet,
Seem then a golden court-way of the Sun!

♦

Why Silent?

WHY am I silent from year to year?
   Needs must I sing on these blue March days?
What will you say, when I tell you here,
   That already, I think, for a little praise,
      I have paid too dear?

For, I know not why, when I tell my thought,
   It seems as though I fling it away;
And the charm wherewith a fancy is fraught,
   When secret, dies with the fleeting lay
      Into which it is wrought.

So my butterfly-dreams their golden wings
But seldom unfurl from their chrysalis;
And thus I retain my loveliest -things,
While the world, in its worldliness, does not miss
What a poet sings.

◆

A Common Thought

Somewhere on this earthly planet
In the dust of flowers to be,
In the dewdrop, in the sunshine,
Sleeps a solemn day for me.

At this wakeful hour of midnight
I behold it dawn in mist,
And I hear a sound o' sobbing
Through the darkness! hist! oh, hist!

In a dim and murky chamber,
I am breathing life away;
Some one draws a curtain softly,
And I watch the broadening day.

As it purples in the zenith,
As it brightens on th lawn,
There's a hush of death about me,
And a whisper, "He s gone!"

◆

The Arctic Voyager

Shall I desist, twice baffled? Once by land,
And once by sea, I fought and strove with storms,
All shades of danger, tides, and weary calms;
Head-currents, cold and famine, savage beasts,
And men more savage; all the while my face
Looked northward toward the pole; if mortal strength
Could have sustained me, I had never turned.
Till I had seen the star which never sets
Freeze in the Arctic zenith. That I failed
To solve the mysteries of the ice-bound world,
Was not because I faltered in the quest.
Witness those pathless forests which conceal
The bones of perished comrades, that long march,
Blood-tracked o'er flint and snow, and one dread night
By Athabasca, when a cherished life
Flowed to give life to others. This, and worse,
I suffered —let it pass — it has not tamed
My spirit nor the faith which was my strength.
Despite of waning years, despite the world
Which doubts, the few who dare, I purpose now —
A purpose long and thoughtfully resolved,
Through all its grounds of reasonable hope—
To seek beyond the ice which guards the Pole,
A sea of open water; for I hold,
Not without proofs, that such a sea exists,
And may be reached, though since this earth was made
No keel hath ploughed it and to mortal ear
No wind hath told its secrets . . . . With this tide

I sail; if all be well, this very moon
Shall see my ship beyond the southern cape
Of Greenland, and far up the bay through which,
With diamond spire and gorgeous pinnacle,
The fleets of winter pass to warmer seas.
Whether, my hardy shipmates ! we shall reach
Our bourne, and come with tales of wonder back,
Or whether we shall lose the precious time,
Locked in thick ice, or whether some strange fate
Shall end us .all, I know not; but I know
A lofty hope, if earnestly pursued,
Is its own crown, and never in this life
Is labour wholly fruitless. In this faith
I shall not count the chances — sure that all
A prudent foresight asks we shall not want,
And all that bold and patient hearts can do
Ye will not leave undone. The rest is God's!

◆

A Vision of Poesy (excerpt)

All lovely things, and gentle—the sweet laugh
Of children, Girlhood's kiss, and Friendship's clasp,
The boy that sporteth with the old man's staff,
The baby; and the breast its fingers grasp —
All that exalts the grounds of happiness,
All griefs that hallow, and all joys that bless,
To me are sacred; at holy shrine
Love breathes its latest dreams, its earliest hints;
I turn life's tasteless waters into wine,

And flush them through and through with purple tints.
Wherever Earth is fair, and Heaven looks down,
I rear my altars, and I wear my crown.

◆

Song

(Composed for Washington's birthday, and respectfully inscribed to the
officers and members of the Washington Light Infantry of' Charleston,
February 22, 1859.)

A hundred years and more ago
A little child was born—
To-day, with pomp of martial show,
We hail his natal morn.

Who guessed as that poor infant wept
Upon a woman's knee,
A nation from the centuries stept
As weak and frail as he?

Who saw the future on his brow
Upon that happy morn?
We are a mighty nation now
Because that child was born.

To him, and to his spirit's scope,
Besides a glorious home,
We owe that what we have and hope
Are more than Greece and Rome.

◆

Hymn

(Sung at the consecration of Magnolia Cemetery, Charleston, S.C.)

Whose was the hand that painted thee, O Death!
    In the false aspect of a ruthless foe,
Despair and sorrow waiting on thy breath —
    O gentle Power! Who could have wronged thee so?

Thou rather shouldst be crowned with fadeless flowers,
    Of lasting fragrance and celestial hue
Or be thy couch amid funereal bowers,
    But let the stars and sunlight sparkle through.

So, with these thoughts before us, we have fixed
    And beautified, O Death I thy mansion here,
Where gloom and gladness —grave and garden mixed,
    Make it a place to love, and not to fear.

◆ ◆ ◆

PAUL HAMILTON HAYNE (1830 — 1886) of South Carolina. Hayne was a romantic poet whose greatest popularity came during and after The War. These are some of his antebellum verses. Yankee bombardment of Charleston destroyed his historic family home and library in Charleston, and he lived thereafter in a cabin in the woods near Augusta, Georgia.

Lines

(Written on Christmas-day, 1853, which fell upon the Sabbath.)

MYSTERY of mysteries! on this holy morn,
The Prince of an eternal realm of love,
The Godhead veiled, in lowliest guise was born,
While the far heavenly music pealed above.

Triumph of triumphs! this auspicious day,
The stern earth-agony subdued, and fled,
Beheld the dawn of his immortal sway,
The glorious resurrection from the dead.

In the long cycles that the years have run,
The course of their majestical advance,
Hath merged with solemn wedlock into one,
These sacred days' sublime significance.

The birth that oped to man the heavenly gate,
And gave far glimpses of supernal light,
The glory of that distant, fair estate,
Faded so long from his despondent sight;

That birth was marvelous! but strange and grand,
More strange and grand was the great Conqueror's rise

From the dim confines of the shadowy land,
Whose gloom had palsied faith, and dimmed the skies.

Thus did the mortal learn immortal trust,
Spurn the base ends for which his soul had striven,
Shake from his garment earth's degrading dust,
And hail a home and brotherhood in Heaven.

◆

My Father

MY FATHER! in the mist-enshrouded Past,
My boyish thoughts have wandered o'er and o'er
To thy lone grave upon a distant shore,
The wanderer of the waters, still at last.

Never in boyhood have I blithely sprung
To catch my father's voice, or climb his knee;
He was a constant Pilgrim of the sea,
And died upon it when his boy was young.

He perished not in conflict nor in flame,
No laurel garland rests upon his tomb;
Wild were his days, and clouded was his doom,
Brief was his life, forgotten is his name.

Yet have I shrined his memory in my mind,
Yet have I wrought his image on my soul—
Though fancy-painted, a most perfect whole
Of sweet conceptions, deep, though dim-defined.

His careless bearing, and his manly face,
His frank, bold eye, his stern and stalworth form
Fitted to breast the' fight, the wreck, the storm;
The sailor's nonchalance, the soldier's grace.

In dreams, in dreams we've mingled, and a swell
Of felling mightier for the eye's eclipse,
The music of a blest Apocalypse,
Hath murmured through my spirit, like a spell.

Ah, then! of times sadder scene will rise,
A gallant vessel through the mist-bound day,
Lifting her spectral spars above the bay,
Swayed gloomily against the glimmering skies.

O'er the dim billows thundering, peals a boom
Of the deep gun that bursteth as a knell,
When the brave tender to the brave farewell—
And strong arms bear a comrade to the tomb.

The opened sod: a sorrowing band beside—
One rattling roll of musketry, and then,
A man no more among his fellow-men,
Darkness his chamber, and the earth his bride.

My father sleeps peace; perchance more blest
Than some he left to mourn him, and to know
The bitter blight of an enduring wo,
Longing (how oft!) with him, to be at rest.

She whom his love sustained, the widowed one,
Is living still, but her promised years
Have floated o'er gloomy gulf of tears,
Illumined not by starlight, nor by sun.

And I, who should have been her age's stay,
Strewing the mourner's rugged road with flowers,
The music of her life's declining hours—
I have but darkened all her desolate way.

And not I know the Pilgrim's path is trod;
A season more, and the celestial Gate
Will open for her, where the angels wait,
To bear the 'heavy laden' up to God.

And when thus goest, sweet mother! and the gleams
From sapphire thrones are round thy footsteps spread;
When the last offspring of thy Grief is dead,
Plead for me there, by the Eternal streams:—

For it may be a stronger, purer light,
From the far confines of that saintly clime,
Shall pour upon the dreary paths of time,
And the wronged human heart be judged aright.

Then, hand in hand with Him, thy spirit's Lord,
Thine earthly lover, and thy heavenly friend,
Will the Immortal for the Mortal bend,
And pray I too may share thy great reward.

♦

Aspiration

To have the will to soar, but not the wings,—
Eyes fixed forever on a starry height,
Where stately shapes of grand imaginings
Flash down the splendors of imperial light;

And yet to lack the charm that makes them ours,
Th' obedient vassals of that conquering spell,
Whose omnipresent and ethereal powers,
Encircle Heaven, nor fear to enter Hell;

This is the doom of Tantalus—the thirst
For beauty's balmy front to quench the fires
Of the wild passion that our soul hath nurst
In hopeless promptings—unfulfilled desires.

Yet would I rather in the outward state
Of Song's immortal Palace lay me down,
A beggar asking by that golden gate,
Than bend beneath the haughtiest Empire's crown.

For sometimes, through the bars, my tranced eyes
Have caught the vision of a life divine,
And seen a far, mysterious rapture rise
Beyond the veil that guard the inmost shrine.

◆

Sonnet — Poets

Some thunder on the heights of song, their race
Godlike in power, while others at their feet
Are breathing measures scarce less strong and sweet
Than those that peal from out that loftiest place;
Meantime, just midway on the mount, his face
Fairer than April heavens, when storms retreat,
And on their edges rain and sunshine meet,
Pipes the soft lyrist lays of tender grace;
But where the slopes of bright Parnassus sweep
Near to the common ground, a various throng
Chant lowlier measures—yet each tuneful strain
(The silvery minor of earth's perfect song)
Blends with that music of the topmost steep,
O'er whose vast realm the master minstrels reign!

♦

The Pine's Mystery

Listen! the somber foliage of the Pine
A swart Gitana of the woodland trees,
Is answering what we may but half divine,
To those soft whispers of the twilight breeze!

Passion and mystery murmur through the leaves,
Passion and mystery, touched by deathless pain,
Whose monotone of long, low anguish grieves
For something that shall not live again!

♦

Aspects of the Pines

Tall somber, grim, they stand with dusky gleams
Brightening to gold within the woodland's core,
Beneath the gracious noontide's tranquil beams—
But the weird winds of morning sigh no more.

A stillness, strange, divine, ineffable,
Broods round and o'er them in the wind's surcease,
And on each tinted copse and shimmering dell
Rests the mute rapture of deep-hearted peace.

◆

Lines

A tender word outspoken,
A tender glance returned
And thoughtless peace was broken,
And quenchless passion burned.

Thenceforth, forever after,
Shadows filled her eyes,
And a low, sad laughter,
Like the sweet uprise
Of melodious fountains
'Mid the Elf-land mountains,
Fell from her, in seeming
Of enraptured dreaming,
Caught from tranced skies.

How the holy story,

Her deep heart's mystery,

Like a chastened glory,

Beautiful to see,

Shone forth, softly, faintly,

With a radiance saintly,

From each pensive feature—

[Oh! divinest Nature,

Once bound up in me!]

Well do I remember

That fair Italian face,

But a drear December

Hath eclipsed its grace;

December of the stormy scorn,

Of folly and of madness born,

That season of infuriate weather,

When Love and Hope went down together.

♦

Stanzas To J. S.

WHEN Darkness encompassed my senses and soul,

And the breath of the Pestilence over me stole,

When the eyes of the Fearful looked misty and dim,

When Love breathed a prayer, and Devotion a hymn,

When the clouds of the Present around me unfurled,

And my glance like a spirit's was turned from the world;

There was One, and scarce less than a spirit was she,

Whose smile fell upon me like light on the sea —

And bore back the waves of my fate as they rolled,
Where Eternity's Day-star just bathed them in gold.
All else were desponding—all else were in tears;
From beneath me seemed gliding the Threshold of years,
A rest—as of death brooded sad o'er the room,
And the low air was heavy with sickly perfume;
The Destroyer's wan scepter o' ershadowed my heart,
And I thought that the Angels stood gazing apart,
And signed me to come, but an Angel more dear,
All bright with mortality's sweetness, was near,
And I turned from the beauty of Adenne to see,
Life, Hope, and Passion, brought earthward by thee.

♦

To

(This is perhaps a tribute to Henry Timrod.)

THY life hath been a warfare from the first,
But one by one thou hast besieged and burst
The iron gates of Prejudice, and wrung
Tardy confession from an enemy's tongue,
Of the just might of genius and of will,
Against their petty instruments of ill—
The sneer of ignorance, and the scorn of pride,
The blinded, arrogant folly that would ride
Rough-shod o'er merit, and the pomp of place
That fain would deem it somewhat of disgrace
To bend its shallow dignity—and know
It doth receive an honour, not bestow,
When one whom God hath gifted with the dower

Of lofty foresight, and rich words of power,
Accepts that homage which a luminous Fate
Decrees the Small must render to the Great.
At last upon thy brow, despite of them,
Fame sets her broad, imperial diadem,
And not a jewel blazes in that crown,
But gleams a separate scorn to quail them down.

♦

This Too, Shall Pass Away

Art thou in misery, brother? Then I pray
Be comforted. Thy grief shall pass away.
Art thou elated? Ah, be not too gay;
Temper thy joy: this, too, shall pass away.
Art thou in danger? Still let reason sway,
And cling to hope: this, too, shall pass away.
Tempted art thou? In all thine anguish lay
One truth to heart: this, too, shall pass away.
Do rays of loftier glory round thee play?
Kinglike art thou? This, too, shall pass away!
Whate'er thou art, wher'er thy footsteps stray,
Heed these wise words: This, too, shall pass away.

♦ ♦ ♦

WILLIAM RUSSELL SMITH (1815 — 1896) of Alabama was a lawyer and U.S. and Confederate congressman, a Confederate colonel, and for a short period president of the University of Alabama. Throughout his long life he was also a devoted writer. Smith in 1833 wrote the first book of poetry published in Alabama and shortly afterward the first play professionally acted in the State. "Solitude of Mind" seems to have been written in 1860 on the eve of secession, which Smith voted against. The lost Pleiad was one of the seven sisters of that star constellation who is said to have come to earth and married a mortal. The poem refers to the one star State flag that was present at the time of secession but was later replaced.

Solitude of Mind

. . . But not alone the Solitude I sing

Of desolate islands and serene retreats

Where genius with the Gods may meditate:

I sing the Solitude of Mind; the power

To draw the sense from its accustomed use

Of natural avenues; the power to be

Still in the uproar, deaf to all the shouts

Of angered multitudes; the power divine

To pluck from turbulence the time to think;

To shape the glowing thoughts to themes sublime

And meditate perfections infinite;

While Fury raves and mobs tumultuous reign.

I held a festival myself, last night;

In my own closet, with my books alone.

My little chamber thronged with visitors.

Some were the spirits of antiquity;

Those demi-gods that walk the dusty realms

Of dim Tradition; mystic forms that grace

The niches of the old world's Pantheon—
And others of a giant race who came,
Grateful to greet their masters; Poets came,
Fresh from Olympian sports, with bays yet green
And flowers unwilted by the century suns;
Came warriors storming from the battlefields,
With dinted shields and foreheads darkly gashed.
O these were glorious guests; Milton was there,
And seemed that he would let me touch his robe!

♦

The Lost Pleiad Found
Sonnet To The Alabama Flag

Long years ago, at night, a female star
Fled from amid the Spheres, and through the space
Of Ether, onward, in a flaming car,
Held, furious, headlong, her impetuous race:
She burnt her way through skies; the azure haze
Of Heaven assumed new colors in her blaze;
Sparklets, emitted from her golden hair,
Diffused rich tones through the resounding air;
The neighboring stars stood mute, and wondered when
The erring sister would return again:
Through Ages still they wondered in dismay;
But now, behold, careering on her way,
The long lost PLEIAD! lo! she takes her place
On ALABAMA'S FLAG, and lifts her radiant face.

♦ ♦ ♦

WILLIAM GILMORE SIMMS (1806 — 1870) of South Carolina, amazingly prolific novelist, poet, essayist, lecturer, historian, critic, and editor, has been rightly called "The Father of Southern Literature." Without question Simms is the most important Southern writer of the 19th century after Poe. Without question Simms is in every way one of the most important American writers. It is a scandal that Boston and New York critics have left him out of the canon. Fortunately, a superb edition of Simms's verse, selected and edited by James E. Kibler, has been published with almost 200 worthwhile poems. Only a small sample can be offered here that seeks to indicate Simms's range of thought and mastery. More Simms will appear in Confederate Poets and Poems.

The Poet

Thou art a Poet, and thy aim has been

To draw from every thought, and every scene

Psychal, and natural, that serene delight

Wherewith our God hath made his words so bright,

The sense of Beauty—the immortal thrill

Of intuitions throned above our Will—

The secret of that yearning, dim, but strong

Which yields the pulse to Hope—the wings to Song.

♦

Shakespeare

The mighty master in each page we trace,

Natural always, never common-place;

Forever frank and cheerful, even when woe,

Commands the sigh to speak, the tear to flow;

Sweet without weakness, without storming, strong,

Jest not too strain'd, nor argument too long;

Still true to reason, though intent on sport,
Thy wit ne'er drives thy wisdom out of court;—
A brooklet now, a noble stream anon,
Careering in the daylight and the sun;
A mighty ocean next, broad, deep and wide,
Earth, sun and heaven, all imaged in its tide!—
Oh! when the master bends him to his art,
How the mind follows, how vibrates the heart,
The mighty grief o'ercomes us as we hear,
And the soul hurries, hungering, to the ear;
The willing nature worships as he sings,
And heaven is won when Genius spreads her wings.

◆

Carolina Woods

These woods have all been haunted, and the power
Of spirits still abides in tree and flower;
They have their tiny elves that dance by night,
When the leaves sparkle in the moonbeam's light;
And the wild Indian often, as he flew
Along their water in his birch canoe,
Beheld, in the soft light of summer eves,
Strange eyes and faces peering through the leaves;
Nor, are they vanish'd yet.—The woodman sees,
Even now, wild forms that lurk behind the trees;
And the pine forests have a chanted song,
The Indians say, must linger in them long.

◆

Religious Musings

The mighty and the massy of the wood
Compel my worship: satisfied I lie,
With nought in sight but forest, earth, and sky,
And give sweet sustenance to precious mood!—
Tis thus from visible but inanimate things,
We gather mortal reverence. They declare
In silence, a persuasion we must share,
Of hidden sources, spiritual springs,

Fountains of deep intelligence, and powers,
That man himself implores not; and I grow
From wonder into worship, as the show,
Majestic, but unvoiced, through noteless hours,
Imposes on my soul, with musings high,
That, like Jacob's Ladder, lifts them to the sky!

♦

Ashley River

Still, still, thou gentle river,
   A long, a last farewell:
I fly from thee forever,
   In other climes to dwell;
And never more, thus roving,
   Along thy banks, shall I,
Behold a stream so worthy loving,
   Beneath the blessed sky.

Thou hast bless'd me with a beauty
  Like a smile from the Most High;
Thou hast cheer'd me with a murmur
  Of music melting by-
I have seen thee in thy glory,
  When the loved ones saw thee too,
But we see them now no longer;
  To them and thee, adieu.

Sad parting with thy waters,
  Sweet waters of my youth;
When every hour was gladness,
  When every tone was truth —
Dark clouds have come about me,
  Thou, too, hast felt the change,
Arid thy billows only flout me,
  With a murmur stern and strange.

Yet, well my heart has loved thee,
  And, alas! it loves thee still;
It cannot soon forget thee,
  Let me roam where'er I will —
Thou still art to my spirit,
  Like a smile from the Most
High — Thou art still most worthy loving
  Beneath the blessed sky

◆

The Fate of the Republics

Thus, the grand fabric of a thousand years—
Rear'd with such art and wisdom by a race
Of giant sires, in virtue all compact,
Self-sacrificing; having grand ideals
Of public strength, and peoples capable
Of great conceptions for the common good,
And of enduring liberties, kept strong
Through purity;— tumbles and falls apart,
Lacking cement in virtue; and assail'd
Within, without, by greed or avarice,
And vain ambition for supremacy.

So fell the old Republics—Gentile and Jew,
Roman and Greek—such evermore the record;
Mix'd glory and shame, still lapsing into greed,
From conquest and from triumph, into fall!
The glory that we see exchanged for guilt
Might yet be glory. There were pride enough,
And emulous ambition to achieve,—
Both generous powers, when coupled With endowment,
To do the work of States—and there were courage
And sense of public need, and public welfare,—
And duty—in a brave but scattered few,
Throughout the States—had these been credited
To combat 'gainst the popular appetites.
But these were scorn'd and set aside for naught,
As lacking favour with the popular lusts
They found reward in exile or in death!

And he alone who could debase his spirit,
And file his mind down to the basest nature
Grew capp'd with rule!—

So, with the lapse
From virtue, the great nation forfeits all
The pride with the security—the liberty,
With that prime modesty which keeps the heart
Upright, in meek subjection, to the doubts
That wait upon Humanity, and teach
Humility, as best check and guaranty,
Against the wolfish greed of appetite!
Worst of all signs, assuring coming doom,
When peoples loathe to listen to the praise
Of their great men; and, jealous of just claims,
Eagerly set upon them to revile,
And banish from their councils! Worse than all
When the great man, succumbing to the mass,
Yields up his mind as a low instrument
To vulgar forgers, to be played upon: —
Yields to the vulgar lure, the cunning bribe
Of place or profit; and makes sale of States
To Party!

Thus and then are States subdued—
'Till one vast central tyranny upstarts,
With front of glittering brass, but legs of clay;
Insolent, reckless of account as right,—
While dust grows license, and tears off the robes

From justice; and makes right a thing of mock;
And puts a foolscap on the head of law,
And plucks the baton of authority
From his right hand, and breaks it o'er his head.

So rages still the irresponsible power,
Using the madden'd populace as hounds,
To hunt down freedom where she seeks retreat.
The ancient history becomes the new—
The ages move in circles, and the snake
Ends ever with his tail in his own mouth.
Thus still in all the past!—and man the same
In all the ages—a poor thing of passion,
Hot greed, and miserable vanity,
And all infirmities of lust and error,
Makes of himself the wretched instrument
To murder his own hope.

    So empires fall,—
Past, present, and to come—
      There, is no hope
For nations or peoples, once they lapse from virtue
And fail in modest sense of what they are—
Creatures of weakness, whose security
Lies in meek resting on the law of God,
And in that wise humility which pleads
Ever for his guardian watch and Government,
Though men may bear the open signs of rule.

Humility is safety could men learn
The law, "ne sutor ultra crepidam,"
And the sagacious cobbler, at his last,
Content himself with paring leather down
To heel and instep, nicely fitting pants,
in proper adaptation, to the foot,
We might have safety.

        Rightly, to conceive
What's right, and limit the o'erreaching will
To this one measure only, is the whole
Of that grand rule, and wise necessity,
Which only gives us safety.

        Where a State,
Or blended States, or peoples, pass the bounds
Set for their progress, they must topple and fall
Into that gulf of ruin which has swallowed
All ancient Empires, States, Republics; all
Perishing, in like manner, from the selfsame cause!
The terrible conjunction of the event,

Close with the provocation, stands apart,
A social beacon in all histories;
And yet we take no heed, but, still rush on,
Under mixed sway of greed and. vanity,
And like the silly boy with his card-castle,
Precipitate to ruin as we build.

♦

Solace of the Woods

WOODS, waters, have a charm to soothe the ear,
When common sounds have vexed it: when the day
Grows sultry, and the crowd is in thy way,
And working in thy soul much toil and care,
Betake thee to the forest: in the shade
Of pines, and by the side of purling streams
That prattle all their secrets in their dreams,
Unconscious of a listener—unafraid—
Thy soul shall feel their freshening, and the truth
Of nature then, reviving in thy heart,
Shall bring thee the best feelings of thy youth,
When in all natural joys thy joy had part,
Ere lucre and the narrowing toils of trade
Had turned thee to the thing thou wast not made.

♦

The Swamp Fox
(The Song of Marion's Men)

We follow where the Swamp Fox guides,
His friends and merry men are we;
And when the troop of Tarleton rides,
We burrow in the cypress tree.
The turfy hammock is our bed,
Our home is in the red deer's den,
Our roof, the tree-top overhead,
For we are wild and hunted men.

We fly by day and shun its light,
But, prompt to strike the sudden blow,
We mount and start with early night,
And through the forest track our foe,
And soon he hears our chargers leap,
The flashing sabre blinds his eyes,
And ere he drives away his sleep,
And rushes from his camp, he dies.

Free bridle-bit, good gallant steed,
That will not ask a kind caress
To swim the Santee at our need,
When on his heels the foemen press—
The true heart and the ready hand,
The spirit stubborn to be free,
The twisted bore, the smiting brand—
And we are Marion's men, you see.

Now light the fire and cook the meal,
The last, perhaps, that we shall taste;
I hear the Swamp Fox round us steal,
And that's a sign we move in haste.
He whistles to the scouts, and hark!
You hear his order calm and low.
Come, wave your torch across the dark,
And let us see the boys that go.

We may not see their forms again,
God help 'em, should they find the strife!
For they are strong and fearless men,
And make no coward terms for life;
They'll fight as long as Marion bids,
And when he speaks the word to shy,
Then, not till then, they turn their steeds,
Through thickening shade and swamp to fly.

Now stir the fire and lie at ease—
The scouts are gone, and on the brush
I see the Colonel bend his knees,
To take his slumbers too. But hush!
He 's praying, comrades; 'tis not strange;
The man that's fighting day by day
May well, when night comes, take a change,
And down upon his knees to pray.

Break up that hoecake, boys, and hand
The sly and silent jug that's there;
I love not it should idly stand
When Marion's men have need of cheer.
'Tis seldom that our luck affords
A stuff like this we just have quaffed,
And dry potatoes on our boards
May always call for such a draught.

Now pile the brush and roll the log;
Hard pillow, but a soldier's head
That's half the time in brake and bog
Must never think of softer bed.
The owl is hooting to the night,
The cooter crawling o'er the bank,
And in that pond the flashing light
Tells where the alligator sank.

What! 'tis the signal! start so soon,
And through the Santee swamp so deep,
Without the aid of friendly moon,
And we, Heaven help us! half asleep!
But courage, comrades! Marion leads,
The Swamp Fox takes us out to-night;
So clear your swords and spur your steeds,
There's goodly chance, I think, of fight.

We follow where the Swamp Fox guides,
We leave the swamp and cypress tree,
Our spurs are in our coursers' sides,
And ready for the strife are we.
The Tory camp is now in sight,
And there he cowers within his den;
He hears our shouts, he dreads the fight,
He fears, and flies from Marion's men.

♦

[No American writer, including James Fenimore Cooper, ever had more understanding, knowledge, and sympathy for the Native Americans than did Simms. They appear in many of his works of poetry and fiction.]

The Green Corn Dance

Come hither, hither, old and young—the gentle and the strong,

And gather in the green corn dance, and mingle with the song—

The summer comes, the summer cheers, and with a spirit gay,

We bless the smiling boon she bears, and thus her gifts repay.

Eagle from the mountain,

Proudly descend!

Young dove from the fountain,

Hitherward bend-

Bright eye of the bower—

Bird, and bud, and flower,—

Come—while beneath the summer's sunny glance,

The green leaf peeps from earth, and mingle in the dance.

Not now reluctant do we come to gladden in the boon,

The gentle summer brings us now, so lavishly and soon-

From every distant village, and from deep secluded glen,

They gather to the green corn dance, bright maids and warrior men.

Of the grave, the gravest,

Smiling, now come-

Of the brave, the bravest

Give the brave room.
Loftiest in station, Sweetest of the nation,

Come—while beneath the summer's sunny glance,
The green blade peeps from earth, and mingle in the dance.

Now give the choral song and shout, and let the green woods ring,
And we will make a merry rout to usher in the spring—
Sing high, and while the happy mass in many a ring goes round,
The birds shall cheer, the woods shall hear, and all the hills
resound.

Fathers, who have taught us
Ably our toil,
For the blessing brought us,
Share with us the spoil.
Spirit-God above us,
Deign thou still to love us,

While long beneath the summer's sunny glance,
We see the green corn spring from earth, and gather in the dance.

♦

Sonnet—The Age of Gold

These times deserve no song—they but deride
The poet's holy craft,—nor his alone;
Methinks as little courtesy is shown
To what was chivalry in days of pride:
Honour but meets with mock:—the worldling shakes
His money-bags, and cries—"My strength is here;
O'er throws my enemy, his empire takes,
And makes the ally serve, the alien fear!"
Is love the object? Cash is conqueror,—
Wins hearts as soon as empires—puts his foot
Upon the best affections, and will spur
His way to eloquence, when Faith stands mute;
And for Religion,—can we hope for her,
When love and valor serve the same poor brute!

♦

Sonnet—Popular Misdirection

Would we recall our virtues and our peace?
The ancient teraphim we must restore;
Bring back the household gods we loved of yore,
And bid our yearning for strange idols cease.
Our worship still is in the public way,—

Our altars are the market-place;—our prayer
Strives for meet welcome in our neighbor's ear,
And heaven affects us little while we pray.
We do not call on God, but man, to hear;—

Nor even on his affections;—we have lost
The sweet humility of our home desires,
And flaunt in foreign fashions at rare cost;
Nor God our souls, nor man our hearts inspires,
Nor aught that should to God or man be dear.

◆

The Decay of a People

This the true sign of ruin to a race—
It undertakes no march, and, day by day
Drowses in camp, or, with the laggard's pace,
Walks sentry o'er possessions that decay;
Destined, with sensible waste, to fleet away;—
For the first secret of continued power
Is the continued conquest;—all our sway
Hath surety in the uses of the hour;
If that we waste, in vain wall'd town and lofty tower!

◆

Song of the South

Oh, the South! the sunny, sunny South!
   Land of true feeling, land forever mine;
I drink the kisses of her rosy mouth,
   And my heart swells as with a draught of wine!
She brings me blessings of maternal love—
   I have her praise which sweetens all my toil;
Her voice persuades her loving smiles approve—
   She sings me from the sky and from the soil!
Oh! by her lonely pines that wave and sigh—
   Oh! by her myriad flowers that bloom and fade;
By all the thousand beauties of her sky,
   And the sweet solemn of her forest shade—
   She's mine, forever mine!
   Nor will I aught resign
Of what she gives me, mortal or divine;
   Will sooner part
   With life—hope—heart—
Will die—before I fly!

Oh! Love is hers, such love as ever glows
   In souls where leaps affection's living tide;
She is all fondness to her friends;—to foes
   She glows a thing of passion, strength and pride!
She feels no tremors when the Danger's nigh;
   But the fight over, and the victory won,
How, with strange fondness, turns her loving eye,
   In tearful welcome, on each gallant son!

Oh! By her virtues of the cherished past—
    By all her hopes of what the future brings—
I glory that my lot with her is cast,
    And my soul flushes, and exultant sings
    She's mine, forever mine!
    For her I will resign
All precious things —all placed upon her shrine;
    Will freely part
    With life—hope—heart—
Will die!—do aught but fly!

◆

The Edge Of The Swamp

'Tis a wild spot, and even in summer hours,
With wondrous wealth of beauty and a charm
For the sad fancy, hath the gloomiest look,
That awes with strange repulsion. There, the bird
Sings never merrily in the sombre trees,
That seem to have never known a term of youth,
Their young leaves all being blighted. A rank growth
Spreads venomously round, with power to taint;
And blistering dews await the thoughtless hand
That rudely parts the thicket. Cypresses,
Each a great ghastly giant, eld and gray,
Stride o'er the dusk, dank tract with buttresses
Spread round, apart, not seeming to sustain,

Yet link' d by secret twines, that, underneath,
Blend with each arching trunk. Fantastic vines,
That swing like monstrous serpents in the sun,
Bind top to top, until the encircling trees
Group all in close embrace. Vast skeletons
Of forests, that hale perish'd ages gone,
Moulder, in mighty masses, on the plain;
Now buried in some dark and mystic tarn,
Or sprawl'd above it, resting on great arms,
And making, for the opossum and the fox,
Bridges, that help them as they roam by night.
Alternate stream and lake, between the banks,
Glimmer in doubtful light: smooth, silent, dark,
They tell not what they harbor; but, beware!
Lest, rising to the tree on which you stand,
You sudden see the moccasin snake heave up
His yellow shining belly and flat head
Of burnish'd copper. Stretch'd at length, behold
Where yonder Cayman, in his natural home,
The mammoth lizard, all his armor on,
Slumbers half-buried in the sedgy grass,
Beside the green ooze where he shelters him,
The place, so like the gloomiest realm of death,
Is yet the abode of thousand forms of life—
The terrible, the beautiful, the strange—
Winged and creeping creatures, such as make
The instinctive flesh with apprehension crawl,

When sudden we behold. Hark! at our voice
The whooping crane, gaunt fisher in these realms,
Erects his skeleton form and shrieks in flight,
On great white wings. A pair of summer ducks,
Most princely in their plumage, as they hear
His cry, with senses quickening all to fear,
Dash up from the lagoon with marvelous haste,
Following his guidance. See! aroused by these,
And startled by our progress o'er the stream,
The steel jaw'd Cayman, from his grassy slope,
Slides silent to the slimy green abode,
Which is his province. You behold him now,
His bristling back uprising as he speeds
To safety, in the centre of the lake,
Whence his head peers alone—a shapeless knot,
That shows no sign of life; the hooded eye,
Nathless, being ever vigilant and sharp,
Measuring the victim. See! a butterfly,
That, traveling all the day, has counted climes
Only by flowers, to rest himself a while,
And, as a wanderer in a foreign land,
To pause and look around him ere he goes,
Lights on the monster's brow. The surly mute
Straightway goes down; so suddenly, that he,
The dandy of the summer flowers and woods,
Dips his light wings, and soils his golden coat,
With the rank waters of the turbid lake.

Wondering and vex' d, the plumed citizen
Flies with an eager terror to the banks,
Seeking more genial natures—but in vain.
Here are no gardens such as he desires,
No innocent flowers of beauty, no delights
Of sweetness free from taint. The genial growth
He loves, finds here no harbor. Fetid shrubs,
That scent the gloomy atmosphere, offend
His pure patrician fancies. On the trees,
That look like felon spectres, he beholds
No blossoming beauties; and for smiling heavens,
That flutter his wings with breezes of pure balm,
He nothing sees but sadness—aspects dread,
That gather frowning, cloud and fiend in one,
As if in combat, fiercely to defend
Their empire from the intrusive wing and beam.
The example of the butterfly be ours.
He spreads his lacquer' d wings above the trees,
And speeds with free flight, warning us to seek
For a more genial home, and couch more sweet
Than these drear borders offer us to-night.

♦

Southern Ode
(1850)

Once more the cry of Freedom peals,
    From broad Potomac's wave to ours,
The invader's cunning footstep steals,
    Usurping fast our rights and powers.
He proffers love, he prates of ties
    That still should bind our fates in one,
Yet weaves his subtle web of lies,
    To share and leave us all undone.
What bond of faith, however strong,
    Thus taught by lust of pelf and sway,
He would not, in his march of wrong,
    Hurl scornful from his treacherous way?
The bond that's sacred in our sight,
    Made pliant by his arts of shame,
Is but the means to rob of right,
    The race he cannot rob of fame!
But we have seen the serpent's trail,
    Have heard the wolf 's base howl, and now,
Taught by the past, we cannot fail,
    To brand his blackness on his brow.
To crush the viper in his path,
Beat down the were-wolf in our wrath,
And severing bonds so idly known,
Strike, though we stand and strike alone!

Oh! they are brethren these, who seek
    To weave their snares about our feet;—
Their prayers how bland, their pleas how meek,
    Most philanthropic all, and sweet!
We see their guile, and when we cry,
    In scorn and anger, at each wrong,
How Christianly they answer —"Fie!"—
    "Brethren!" the burden of their song!
We show our bonds of union broke,
    Each shatter'd tie, each sunder'd string,
And toiling still our necks to yoke,
    How well of "Union" do they sing!
This marriage bond they plead, while still
    In most adulterous arts they strive;
On us bestow its fruits of ill,
    While they on all its profits thrive.
Their bondmen we, who wage the fight,
    Achieve the spoil and win the day;
They, the keen knaves, with trick of sleight,
    The danger o'er, to steal the prey!
Thus, upon Sinbad's back astride,
The Old Man of the Sea would ride,
While preaching, ever and anon,
"Still let us ride together, son!"

Throw by the Harp! 'tis mockery now—
    Decree that dance and revel cease;

The shame spot darkens on your brow,
    And death is in the snares of peace!
It mocks the past our fathers knew;
    To sing the oppressions we must bear;
To swords, not songs, they bravely flew,
    And broke the very chains we wear.
They only felt the wrong, to spring,
    With fury to the desperate fray;
And did not, like their children, cling
    To bonds that crushed their souls to clay.
They too, had ties, long sacred known,
    With loyal hearts they loved the true;
But, when a tyrant filled the throne,
    They trampled throne and tyrant too.
What union firmer knit than theirs,
    With Britain from their earliest hours;
And yet, when Britain moved their fears,
    For freedom, they o'erthrew her powers.
The tie that cunning makes its plea,
To rob the birthright from the free,
Though by our sires with blessings given,
Is fit for Hell, though forged in Heaven!

'Tis peace no more! for peace is rest,
    In mutual faith, so well bestow'd,
That doubt and danger fill no breast,
    And lust and envy never goad.

What hope have we of state like this?
　　Who that has seen the fraudful past,
But feels that still the serpent's hiss,
　　Our hour of dreaming peace must blast.
Our Union still hath been the plea,
　　To strip us of our natural strength,
Our peace—its future ye should see
　　In utter deep despair at length.
A dull, dread wearisome repose,
　　Low crouching still in trembling hush,
In moment fear of bonds and blows,
　　When power feels bold enough to crush!
With, day by day, some birthright lost,
Some pride depress'd, some purpose cross'd,
Cursed with each thought that brings the past,
And utter slaves to knaves at last!

◆ ◆ ◆

About the Editor

DR. CLYDE WILSON is Emeritus Distinguished Professor of History of the University of South Carolina, where he served from 1971 to 2006. He holds a Ph.D. from the University of North Carolina at Chapel Hill. He recently completed editing of a 28-volume edition of *The Papers of John C. Calhoun* which has received high praise for quality. He is author or editor of more than 20 other books and over 700 articles, essays, and reviews in a variety of books and journals, and has lectured all over the U.S. and in Europe, many of his lectures having been recorded online and on CDs and DVDs. Dr. Wilson directed 17 doctoral dissertations, a number of which have been published. Books written or edited include *Why the South Will Survive, Carolina Cavalier: The Life and Mind of James Johnston Pettigrew, The Essential Calhoun*, three volumes of *The Dictionary of Literary Biography* on American Historians, *From Union to Empire: Essays in the Jeffersonian Tradition, Defending Dixie: Essays in Southern History and Culture, Chronicles of the South, Calhoun: A Statesman for the 21st Century, The Yankee Problem*, and *Looking For Mr. Jefferson*. Dr. Wilson is founding director of the Society of Independent Southern Historians; former president of the St. George Tucker Society for Southern Studies; recipient of the Bostick Prize for Contributions to South Carolina Letters, the first annual John Randolph Society Lifetime Achievement Award, and of the Robert E. Lee Medal of the Sons of Confederate Veterans. He is M.E. Bradford Distinguished Professor of the Abbeville Institute; Contributing Editor of *Chronicles: A Magazine of American Culture*; founding dean of the Stephen D. Lee Institute, educational arm of the Sons of Confederate Veterans; and co-founder of Shotwell Publishing.

Dr. Wilson has two grown daughters, an excellent son-in-law, and two outstanding grandsons. He lives in the Dutch Fork of South Carolina, not far from the Santee Swamp where Francis Marion and his men rested between raids on the first invader.

JEFFERY ADDICOTT

*Union Terror: Debunking the
False Justifications for Union Terror*

*Trampling Union Terror:
Riders of the Second Alabama Cavalry*

MARK ATKINS

Women in Combat: Feminism Goes to War

JOYCE BENNETT

*Maryland, My Maryland:
The Cultural Cleansing of a Small Southern State*

GARRY BOWERS

*Slavery and The Civil War:
What Your History Teacher Didn't Tell You*

Dixie Days: Reminiscences Of a Southern Boyhood

JERRY BREWER

Dismantling the Republic

ANDREW P. CALHOUN

*My Own Darling Wife: Letters From A
Confederate Volunteer*

JOHN CHODES

Segregation: Federal Policy or Racism?

*Washington's KKK: The Union League During
Southern Reconstruction*

WALTER BRIAN CISCO

War Crimes Against Southern Civilians

DAVID T. CRUM

Stonewall Jackson: Saved by Providence

JOHN DEVANNY

Continuities: The South in a Time of Revolution

*Lincoln's Continuing Revolution: Essays of M.E.
Bradford and Thomas H. Landess*

JOSHUA DOGGRELL

Doxed: The Political Lynching of a Southern Cop

JAMES C. EDWARDS

*What Really Happened?:
Quantrill's Raid On Lawrence, Kansas*

TED EHMANN

*Boom & Bust In Bone Valley: Florida's
Phosphate Mining History 1886-2021*

JOHN AVERY EMISON

*The Deep State Assassination
of Martin Luther King Jr.*

DON GORDON

*Snowball's Chance: My Kidneys Failed,
My Wife Left Me & My Dog Died...*

JOHN R. GRAHAM

Constitutional History of Secession

PAUL C. GRAHAM

Confederaphobia

*When The Yankees Come: Former Carolina
Slaves Remember*

*Nonsense on Stilts: The Gettysburg Address
& Lincoln's Imaginary Nation*

JOE D. HAINES

*The Diary of Col. John Henry Stover Funk
of the Stonewall Brigade, 1861-1862*

CHARLES HAYES

The REAL First Thanksgiving

V.P. HUGHES

Col. John Singleton Mosby: In the News 1862-1916

TERRY HULSEY

25 Texas Heroes

*The Constitution of Non-State Government:
Field Guide to Texas Secession*

JOSEPH JAY

*Sacred Conviction:
The South's Stand for Biblical Authority*

JAMES R. KENNEDY

Dixie Rising: Rules For Rebels

*Nullifying Federal and State Gun Control:
A How-To Guide For Gun Owners*

*When Rebel Was Cool:
Growing Up In Dixie, 1950-1965*

*Reconstruction: Destroying the Republic
and Creating an Empire*

WALTER D. KENNEDY

The South's Struggle: America's Hope

*Lincoln, The Non-Christian President:
Exposing The Myth*

Lincoln, Marx, and the GOP

J.R. & W.D. KENNEDY

*Jefferson Davis: High Road to Emancipation
and Constitutional Government*

*Yankee Empire:
Aggressive Abroad and Despotic at Home*

Punished With Poverty: The Suffering South

The South Was Right! 3rd Edition

LEWIS LIBERMAN

Snowflake Buddies; ABC Leftism For Kids!

PHILIP LEIGH

*The Devil's Town: Hot Springs During
The Gangster Era*

U.S. Grant's Failed Presidency

The Causes of the Civil War

*The Dreadful Frauds: Critical Race Theory
And Identity Politics*

JACK MARQUARDT

*Around The World In 80 Years: Confessions
of a Connecticut Confederate*

MICHAEL MARTIN

Southern Grit: Sensing The Siege at Petersburg

SAMUEL MITCHAM

*The Greatest Lynching In American History:
New York, 1863*

*Confederate Patton: Richard Taylor and
The Red River Campaign*

CHARLES T. PACE

Lincoln As He Really Was

*Southern Independence. Why War? The War
To Prevent Southern Independence*

JAMES R. ROESCH

From Founding Fathers To Fire Eaters

KIRKPATRICK SALE

*Emancipation Hell: The Tragedy Wrought
By Lincoln's Emancipation Proclamation*

JOSEPH SCOTCHIE

*The Asheville Connection:
The Making of a Conservative*

ANNE W. SMITH

Charlottesville Untold: Inside Unite The Right

Robert E. Lee: A History for Kids

KAREN STOKES

A Legion Of Devils: Sherman In South Carolina

*The Burning of Columbia, S.C.: A Review
of Northern Assertions and Southern Facts*

Carolina Love Letters

*Fortunes of War:
The Adventures of a German Confederate*

*A Confederate in Paris:
Letters of A. Dudley Mann 1867-1879*

JOSEPH R. STROMBERG

*Southern Story and Song:
Country Music in the 20th Century*

JACK TROTTER

Last Train to Dixie

JOHN THEURSAM

Key West's Civil War

H.V. TRAYWICK, JR.

*Along The Shadow Line:
A Road Trip through History and Memory
on the Old Confederate Border*

LESLIE TUCKER

*Old Times There Should Not Be Forgotten:
Cultural Genocide In Dixie*

JOHN VINSON

Southerner Take Your Stand!

MARK R. WINCHELL

*Confessions of a Copperhead:
Culture and Politics in the Modern South*

CLYDE N. WILSON

Calhoun: A Statesman for the 21st Century

*Lies My Teacher Told Me: The True History
of the War For Southern Independence*

The Yankee Problem: An American Dilemma

*Annals Of The Stupid Party:
Republicans Before Trump*

*Nullification:
Reclaiming The Consent of the Governed*

The Old South: 50 Essential Books

The War Between The States: 60 Essential Books

*Reconstruction and the New South, 1865-1913:
50 Essential Books*

*The South 20th Century And Beyond:
50 Essential Books*

*Southern Poets and Poems, 1606 -1860:
The Land They Loved, Volume 1*

Looking For Mr. Jefferson

African American Slavery in Historical Perspective

JOE WOLVERTON

*What Degree Of Madness?: Madison's Method
To Make American States Again*

WALTER KIRK WOOD

*Beyond Slavery: The Northern Romantic
Nationalist Origins of America's Civil War*

Green Altar (Literary Imprint)

CATHARINE BROSMAN

*An Aesthetic Education
and Other Stories (2nd Ed)*

Chained Tree, Chained Owls: Poems

Aerosols and Other Poems

RANDALL IVEY

*A New England Romance:
And Other Southern Stories*

SUZANNE JOHNSON

Maxcy Gregg's Sporting Journals 1842-1858

JAMES E. KIBBLER, JR.

Tiller : Clayback County Series, Vol. 4

The Gentler Gamester

*In the Deep Heart's Core: Poems of Tribute and
Remembrance (forthcoming)*

THOMAS MOORE

*A Fatal Mercy:
The Man Who Lost The Civil War*

PERRIN LOVETT

The Substitute, Tom Ironsides 1

KAREN STOKES

Belles

Carolina Twilight

Honor in the Dust

The Immortals

The Soldier's Ghost: A Tale of Charleston

WILLIAM THOMAS

*Runaway Haley:
An Imagined Family Saga*

*The Field of Justice: Moonshine
and Murder in North Georgia*

Gold-Bug
(Mystery & Suspense Imprint)

BRANDI PERRY

Splintered: A New Orleans Tale

MARTIN WILSON

To Jekyll and Hide